KWANT, Remy C.   Phenomenology of Expression.   Duquesne, 1969.
   191p   68-59089. 5.95.   SBN 8207-0108-4

CHOICE   OCT. '70

Philosophy

Kwant explores Merleau-Ponty's idea (from *The Visible and the Invisible*, 1969) "that man makes reality be for himself through his creative act of expression," treating of expression and existence, creative disclosure of being, interiority, playfulness, verbal expression, "actual" problems, and religious expression.   Proceeds reflectively and concretely, handling much subject matter of special concern to young people today.   Despite some stylistic awkwardness, work should be of great interest to many undergraduates and their teachers; obviously, Merleau-Ponty's work is more authoritative, but is is also more difficult, and, in this area, left incomplete at his death.   Index.

PHENOMENOLOGY OF EXPRESSION

PHENOMENOLOGY OF EXPRESSION

by Remy C. Kwant, Ph.D.

DUQUESNE UNIVERSITY PRESS
Pittsburgh, Pa.
Editions E. Nauwelaerts, Louvain

By the same author

PHILOSOPHY OF LABOR, 1960, $5.25

ENCOUNTER, second impression, 1965, $3.25

THE PHENOMENOLOGICAL PHILOSOPHY OF MER-
LEAU-PONTY, 1963, $5.25

PHENOMENOLOGY OF LANGUAGE, 1965, $6.95

PHENOMENOLOGY OF SOCIAL EXISTENCE, 1965,
$5.95

FROM PHENOMENOLOGY TO METAPHYSICS. *An
Inquiry into the Last Period of Merleau-Ponty's
Philosophical Life*, 1966, $7.95

CRITIQUE: *Its Nature and Function*, 1967, $4.95

All published by Duquesne University Press

Library of Congress Catalog Card Number 68–59089
© 1969, by Duquesne University
Printed in the United States of America

Preface

EXPRESSION is a phenomenon which at present occupies much of the attention of those who devote themselves to education. Even in the recent past education seemed to aim primarily at introducing the young to the existing achievements of culture in its broad sense; now, however, the educators also endeavor to awaken the pupil's expressive powers. This is done, for instance, in so-called free expression. The children are given certain materials, placed in a certain situation and then an attempt is made to induce them to express themselves in a free form. The avowed goal is to prevent these children from becoming stereotyped human beings and to help them really become themselves. The conviction underlying these attempts is that every man possesses hidden powers of expression and that the development of these powers is an essential part of man's self-development. Experts today make a serious study of the various forms which man's expressive life can assume.

It is not the philosopher's task to give directives for the development of the various forms expressive life can assume, for such directives need to be formulated by specialists in the various forms of expression. The philosopher, however, is entitled to inquire into the general characteristics of expression and to ask himself what place expression occupies within the whole of human existence.

For it is his task to describe the essential characteristics of human existence, and the fundamental relationship between man and the world. Now, expression undoubtedly is one of these essential characteristics. The aim of this little work, then, is to describe expression as one of man's fundamental characteristics.

Those who are familiar with the author's publications know that his philosophical thinking is primarily inspired by Maurice Merleau-Ponty. The study of this philosopher's works induced the author to reflect upon the phenomenon "expression." Merleau-Ponty's works contain valuable ideas about this phenomenon. For example, his *Phenomenology of Perception* has a chapter entitled "The Body as Expression, and Speech."[1] His posthumous work *The Visible and the Invisible* ends with about one hundred pages of personal notes and some of these pages contain valuable ideas about expression and its relationship to life and the world.[2] Merleau-Ponty's reflections on this matter may be considered the beginning of a philosophy of expression.

Although it is profoundly influenced by him, this book should not be regarded as an historical study of Merleau-Ponty; rather, I would say, it is a study inspired by this French philosopher, one which collects the scattered elements contained in his works and then pursues the same line of thought. I sincerely hope that this study will prove to be useful to those who devote themselves to the development of man's expressive life.

REMY C. KWANT

---

[1] Humanities Press, New York, 1962, pp. 174 ff.

[2] *Le visible et l'invisible*, Gallimard, Paris, 1964; English edition is in preparation.

Preface to English Edition

This work has been translated directly from the author's manuscript by the undersigned. It does not deviate from the original Dutch text, which will appear shortly.

Our thanks are due to the author for personally reading and approving the translation, and to Miss Judith A. Doyle for making a few literary revisions and looking after the consistency of punctuation.

Henry J. Koren

Contents

CHAPTER ONE

Existence and Expression

THOSE WHO expect this philosophical study of expression to begin with a definition will be disappointed. As the very term indicates, a definition always delimitates. Thus there is always a danger that one who begins with a definition will conceive the object of his interest too narrowly. One of the reasons for this first chapter is precisely the intention to avoid this danger. We wish to show how many-sided the phenomenon "expression" is, even though we restrict ourselves to man. Even this very restriction is a limitation, for genuine expressions occur also in the animal world. One can clearly see that a dog joyfully greets his master and approaches the stranger with distrust. According to the almost classical expression of F. J. Buyten-dijk, the animal is a "shadow of man." In the animal we encounter human phenomena in a shadowlike fashion, i.e., animal behavior makes us think of man but, at the same time, this behavior has such a strange character that it is very difficult to describe it. To write in a responsible way about animal expression, one would have to engage first in empirical research: philosophical reflection alone would not be sufficient.

Even if we limit ourselves to man, there is still danger that we will conceive expression too narrowly. For reasons that will be mentioned later, schools and institutes for expression are now coming into existence, and these institutes devote themselves to expressive gestures, speech and artistic endeavors. There are ways of acting whose expressive character is rather obvious and which, therefore, are generally known as expressions. Thus one could propose that certain ways of acting be called "expressions" and that others be denied this name. In other words, expression would be a particular way of man's acting. Prudence, however, is necessary in this matter. One can speak of an expressive, even eloquent look; the way a hungry child eats is a delight to his mother. In other words, we must leave room for the hypothesis that all human activities can have an expressive character.

1. EXPRESSION IS NOT LIMITED TO MAN'S CONSCIOUS LIFE

Verbal expression is undoubtedly the dominant form of expression, and our speech is a conscious activity: we know what we say. Artistic expression also has a conscious character. Must we say, therefore, that expression is always a conscious activity?

It would be dangerous to use here the term "conscious." In former times people too easily opposed the conscious spirit to unconscious nature. Today we speak in a more differentiated way, as is evident from the existence of such terms as preconscious, subconscious and semi-conscious. There is an obvious temptation, one to which many gave in in the past, to use our experience of consciousness in order to form concepts and establish conceptual oppositions and then to project these upon reality. In the conceptual order the opposition between conscious and unconscious seems to be rather obvious. Conscious is that which is known to itself, and unconscious is that which is hidden to itself. Such a sharp opposition, however, is not to be

found in reality. True, it is possible to indicate realities
that are conscious and others that are unconscious. While
smoking, I am conscious that I smoke, but my cigarette is
not conscious of the fact that it is being smoked by me.
But today we know that the conscious is never entirely
conscious.[1] One who is smoking usually knows that he
smokes, but, generally speaking, not why he smokes, why
he is attached to smoking, how this attachment has arisen,
how smoking functions within his entire existence, that
smoking is a pursuit which should be understood within a
certain social context, etc.

Our expression is often, but not always, a conscious
activity. Even when it is a conscious activity, it usually
has also unconscious aspects. Let us begin with these
unconscious aspects. Speech is a striking example of conscious expression: we know that we are speaking and we
know what we are saying. We are responsible for our
spoken expressions: if they hurt or insult someone, we can
be called to account. But, while speaking, we also bring
forward aspects of our existence, or rather of our attitude,
of the way we relate to people and things, which perhaps
we do not at all know. One who is obtrusive will manifest
this quality in his speaking, e.g., by his tone of voice or
the way in which he constantly interrupts the others. If
his obtrusiveness did not manifest itself in his behavior,
the others would not even know about this obnoxious trait.

---

[1] Freud's investigations have greatly contributed to this.
"Freud uses the term 'preconscious' in reference to the entire
field of that which is not actually present in consciousness but
which, if need be, can always be called back to consciousness.
The unconscious, on the other hand, is for him that of which one
cannot become conscious but which, nonetheless, exercises influence in a distorted way because it insistently tries to make
itself felt under various disguises." H. T. Piron, "Het onbewuste,"
Psychoanalyse, wetenschap van de mens, ed. by W. Huber and
others, Nederlandse Boekhandel, Antwerpen, 1966, p. 72.

In many cases, however, the person himself is ignorant of such a quality.

One could say that in our speech a distinction should be made between our speaking as behavior and speaking as the disclosure of certain viewpoints. Thus we would be fully conscious of what we disclose, even if our speaking as behavior has features which are perhaps unknown to us. The existence of such features is beyond doubt: one's way of speaking is pleasant, the other's not; one is modest, the other is obtrusive, one has sex-appeal, the other lacks it. Such features of our speaking are usually not known to us, even though they belong to our speech as expression.

It is too optimistic, however, to assume that we fully know what we are saying when we speak. A child who tells other children that he just got a new little brother does not realize exactly what has happened. For this reason, adults are sometimes amused when they hear children uninhibitedly talking about things whose tenor they cannot yet understand. This phenomenon is, of course, not limited to children. When, in 1789, people all over Europe heard that a revolution had broken out in Paris, they could not fully know what they were telling one another—just as, today, we do not fully know what we are talking about when we discuss the war in Vietnam. If a very critical-minded person were to ask us details whenever we say something, and thereby force us to be very precise, we would often come to the conclusion that we do not exactly know what we are talking about. Anyone occasionally happens to be well-informed about an affair that others discuss: he then realizes that the others do not really know what they are talking about.

What exactly is meant when we say that there will be a shower? We intend to convey that the sky will become overcast and that a certain form of precipitation will fall from the clouds, but this does not mean that we know exactly what a shower is. Similarly, when we tell someone that a friend has become ill, we do not know exactly what this communication means. It can easily happen that our words have for the other a meaning of which we, ourselves, have no inkling. If, for example, I say that so and so has gone to consult a lawyer, one who knows him well may understand that a threatening divorce is one step closer to realization. Anyone of us is likely to have now a fuller understanding of statements which he used to echo in the past. Yet, who can guarantee that he understands them now fully?

Psychiatry is a science which helps us understand part of that which is not understood in human communications. When a patient speaks with the psychiatrist, his words sometimes have a meaning, for the psychiatrist, which they do not have for the patient himself, at least not on a conscious level. The psychiatrist usually listens also to communications which the patient makes when he speaks without being aware of the fact that his words convey more than he knows. He communicates things which he does not directly wish to communicate. For this reason a conversation between a psychiatrist and his patient is only partially a genuine dialog, for the centers of attention do not coincide. If the patient tells him about his dreams, the psychiatrist hears other things than the dreamer thinks he is saying. He would be very much surprised if the psychiatrist explained to him the meaning of his story.

What we say does not *per se* coincide with what we intend to say. One who begins to speak wishes to point out certain things. But his words can have a scope that exceeds his intentions. When, for instance, Adam Smith wrote his *Wealth of Nations*, he intended to plead for freedom of action on the part of the enterprising and investing bourgeois with respect to conservative feudal government authorities. In reality his plea for freedom also made the bourgeois free to rob others of their freedom. There are passages in his book which, in our opinion, allow us to see this unintended implication of Adam Smith's plea.[2] Similarly, Marx did not intend to promote the dictatorship of a small segment of the Party over the entire Party and the People, but there are passages in his works which fostered such a situation.[3]

How does it happen that we can say more than we intend to convey? Our speech does not have its sole source in ourselves: we actively take up the speaking that is going on all around us. In this way, our speech acquires a certain "weight" from our social context, a weight which we do not fully fathom and which we are even unable fully to understand. Two extremes are to be avoided in this matter. On the one hand, we are not blind exponents of a large anonymous whole of discourse: we know what we are saying. On the other, our speaking does not wholly arise from ourselves and is not wholly borne by our own personal insight; for this reason our speech can contain

[2] In particular, those passages in which Smith argues in favor of greater freedom of action for the individual citizen and rejects government's interference. In a later period this freedom would develop into the power to make others unfree.

[3] Writing about the steps to be taken after the proletarian revolution, Marx says: "In the beginning, this cannot be effected except by means of despotic inroads on the rights of property, and on the conditions of bourgeois production; by means of measures, therefore, which appear economically insufficient and untenable" (*Manifesto of the Communist Party*, Moscow, n.d., pp. 88). Marx's intention was to establish "an association, in which the free development of each is the condition for the free development of all" (*ibid.*, p. 90). Experience, however, has shown that the initial despotic inroads do not *per se* lead to the intended freedom and can lead to a permanent dictatorship. Without willing it, Marx's words have fostered this dictatorship. Cf. Henry J. Koren, *Marx and the Authentic Man*, Duquesne University Press, 1968, Chapter Four and Appendix.

more meaning than we ourselves realize. It can easily happen that people who belong to the same community or group strenuously oppose one another and have the feeling that they have nothing in common. Outsiders who listen to the dispute or read the polemical exchange, however, see that what divides the antagonists is of less importance than what unites them. A sharp dispute is usually possible only between people who share a common world of meaning. For these antagonists this common world of meaning is often so obvious and unquestioned that it escapes their attention, but for outsiders, who do not share this unquestioned world of meaning, the common acceptance of this world is often more relevant than the explicit display of antagonism.

In what we say and the way we behave, in play and recreation, science and philosophy, in short, in all our forms of expression, we reveal the spirit of our time according to the fashion of the society to which we belong; yet, we do not know, or at least, we know but very little about the spirit of our era and the way our society expresses itself. Moreover, our expression always has a personal style which, likewise, is not clearly known to us. One who is familiar with Kant or Hegel recognizes them when he reads an extended passage of their work, even if it is reproduced without the author's name: Kant writes like Kant, and Hegel like Hegel. Yet, neither Kant nor Hegel knew clearly what it meant to express themselves like Kant or Hegel.

While expression often is a conscious activity, it is never fully conscious. As should be evident from the preceding paragraphs, there is no abrupt transition from the conscious to the unconscious dimension of our expression. Consciousness is essentially a matter of more or less. We are, besides, able to become conscious of what is unconscious and to raise to a higher degree of consciousness that of which we are already semi-conscious. People who earn their living in a particular form of expression usually must see to it that they refine and improve that form, and this would not be possible if they did not become more conscious of that form. In many cases assiduous training is necessary for this purpose. We use the detour of reflection to improve our expressivity, i.e., instead of involving ourselves in expression, we place ourselves at a distance from it in order to watch and evaluate it.

For example, one who wishes to improve his speaking, will listen to his own voice on a recorder and watch his own gestures on a screen. But he does this for the avowed purpose of subsequently engaging himself more effectively in expression, and when he thus engages himself, he concentrates his attention on the subject matter and no longer on his own expressivity. While we are engaged in expression, we do not usually pay attention to the expression as such. One who does it anyhow, impresses his listeners as a slightly ridiculous cultivator of mannerisms. Our expressivity is subject to improvement, but the improvement must become, as it were, a second nature

2. Hidden Forms of Expression

Even when it is conscious, expression has unconscious dimensions. This fact makes us realize that there are hidden forms of expression, i.e., that even activities which are not normally called "expression" have an expressive character. Let us take seeing as an example. Certain ways of speaking indicate that our seeing has an expressive character, even though it is true that we would not place seeing at the head of a list of examples illustrating expression. We speak, for instance, of an expressive look, an eloquent look, a look that "speaks volumes," a radiant look, a surprised look. The way one looks can tell us whether what we are saying pleases or displeases him. One who is accustomed to public speaking can see by the looks of his audience whether or not they understand him, are interested or bored. One's way of listening can express boredom, arrogance or interest. These and many other expressive features point to the fact that our seeing and hearing have the character of an expressive activity.

Some people may be surprised by this, for it is customary to make a distinction between gathering impressions and our expressive activity. In former times, philosophers distinguished between impressed cognitive images ("impressed species") and expressed cognitive images ("expressed species"). They were usually not aware of the existential, intentional character of man's knowledge, i.e., of the fact that, in knowing, we, as it were, stand outside ourselves to be with the known reality. They conceived knowledge as an activity which ran its course within the knower's interiority. Thus, there arose the problem of how such an interior activity could put us "in touch" with realities outside ourselves. In that conception of knowledge two things were taken for granted: first, that knowing is an interior event; second, that the knower knows things outside himself. Because these two points seemed to be contradictory, an attempt was made to reconcile them by introducing "cognitive images": man has within himself images of the things outside himself, and by means of those images an activity that remains interior can, nonetheless, make him know the external realities. For those cognitive images do not show themselves as images but show that of which they are images. Thus, strange as it may seem, we do not notice those images in our everyday experience, but through reflection we know that they must exist.

A distinction, we said, was made between impressed and expressed images. There is question of impressed images when things impress images of themselves on us. We ourselves do not form them, but we simply receive them from the things. In some cases, however, the cognitive images cannot exist without expressive activity on our part; for example, when we have images of absent things, the things themselves are not present and, therefore, cannot give us any impressions of themselves. The same happens when our images have characteristics which cannot be found in the things themselves. For example, we have a universal idea of particular things: although I see only concrete human beings, I have an idea of man as such. This universal and abstract character of the cognitive image cannot come from the things themselves; hence it must come from man's own expressive activity. With respect to our cognitive images, then, man was supposed to be sometimes expressive and sometimes non-expressive. Thomas Aquinas says, for instance, that we are not expressive with respect to seeing, more generally, with respect to sense perception in general. We merely gather impressions there. But when we recall absent things or understand concrete things in an abstract way, then we are expressive.[4]

We have related this view somewhat at length because it offers an interesting example of a theory which does not recognize the expressive character of certain activities. According to this theory, some activities are expressive, and others are not. In our own view, all of man's activities have an expressive character. It remains meaningful, nev-

----

[4] "In reply to the second objection, the cognitive act of the external sense is performed by the immutation of the sense by the sensible object alone; hence this sense senses through the form which is impressed on it by the sensible object. But the external sense does not form any sensible image for itself. The imaginative power, however, forms such an image, and the 'word of the intellect' is somehow similar to this form" (*Quaestiones quodlibetales*, V, art. 9, *ad* 2).

ertheless, to speak of impressions, even though the term "cognitive images" is not very fortunate. For, obviously, there is an aspect of passivity in our knowledge. When, for example, I glance out of the window, it does not depend upon my own choice whether or not I will see the sun shining or people moving around in my garden. The seen reality imposes itself on me. It happens all too frequently that we see things which we prefer not to see: parents, for example, cannot avoid seeing sooner or later that one of their children is defective, even if at first they refuse to see this. In this respect one can justifiably speak of "impressions." We could also say that in this respect our knowledge has the character of *receiving* the meaning or signification of reality. One who denies this receptive character makes it impossible for himself to understand the nature of the cognitive process and of scientific investigation.

At the same time, however, even our so-called sense perception always has also the character of a *giving* of meaning. As Edgar Rubin points out, our perception always reveals the structure of figure and field, perception always implies that something shows itself as a figure within a field. There is a visual field, a sonorous field, a tactile field, a field of odors and flavors. Whatever is perceived appears within a field. But there is question of perception in the full sense only when within this field something stands out as a figure, a center. When our looking is a genuine looking and not an empty gazing, this implies that something stands out in our visual field, while the rest remains immersed in the field. If, for example, I look at a car in the park, I do not look at the trees, the grass or the fence. I can, of course, switch and begin to look at a tree, but then the car becomes more or less immersed in the vagueness of the visual field. The same applies to every form of perception. If I attentively listen to a speaker, the noise of the city becomes immersed in the sonorous field. I can also try to analyze the city noise that penetrates into the auditorium, but in that case the speaker's voice sinks away into the indeterminateness of the sonorous field and I do no longer listen to him.

All this implies that our perception is structured.[5] Now, the structuralization of the field of perception is not simply imposed on us by reality but has its co-source also in ourselves. To learn to perceive is to learn to structure the field of perception. We do not know whether and to what extent a new-born baby has the power to structure the field of perception, and for this reason we do not know what the baby sees, hears or feels. Adults also have experiences which make it evident that, without structuralization of the visual field, there is no genuine seeing. If, for example, technically illiterate people pay their first visit to a modern factory, or if people who know nothing about automation are allowed to look at the innards of an automated production apparatus, they do not really see anything. They are unable to detach figures from the field, they cannot structure the field and the proper character of all these things escapes them completely. The same applies to the tasting of wine or the smelling of perfume: the non-expert recognizes neither the type of wine nor the kind of perfume. Genuine perception arises only if we are able to structure the field of perception.

We begin to really see because we structure the field of vision. For this reason, we may say that our seeing is a visualizing of reality, i.e., a constituting of its visibility. The world is not a ready-made visual field which lies there before us in reality awaiting to be seen, but we ourselves actively make visible reality visible by structuring the visual field. Man must learn to see.

Let us add that epistemology shows the truth of all this

[5] Following Husserl, phenomenological philosophy generally devotes much attention to the structure of the field of perception.

on an even deeper level than one can deduce from the preceding paragraphs. Man visualizes reality not only by structuring the pregiven visual field but also by the fact that he himself constitutes this visual field. Naive realism thought that the world is of itself a visual field, but critical reflection has made us realize that this is not so. Things are not of and in themselves red, blue or yellow; the world that stretches around us is not a field in which the earth and the sky meet in an horizon. Outside us, there exist no ready-made colors, sounds, odors and flavors. Thus, one can understand why the opposite extreme of complete subjectivism gained adherents when naive realism proved untenable. The idea gained ground that the field of colors, sounds, odors and flavors is wholly and entirely a field of subjective impressions existing within man himself. Outside man, there was supposed to be nothing but stimuli giving rise to these subjective impressions. This subjectivism, however, contradicts our evident experience: reality itself appears to us as a visual field, a sonorous field, etc. Thus we meet here a strange kind of a paradox: on the one hand, the world is not of and in itself a visual field; on the other, it is nonetheless the world itself which becomes a visual field.

The solution of this paradox is both simple and surprising: man himself, in interaction with reality, makes the world appear as a visual field. Seeing is an existential, intentional activity, i.e., a being-busy with things. This being-busy consists in this that we make reality appear as a visual field. We may repeat here, but now in a more profound sense, the formula: our seeing is a visualization. To see is not to appropriate a ready-made present visibility of things but to constitute this visibility. This constitution does not occur in an arbitrary fashion: it does not depend on our fancy that grass is green or a clear sky blue.

All this makes it evident to what extent our seeing is an expressive activity. Through our seeing we actively constitute the world precisely as the field of vision. There is no question of merely receiving impressions, as Thomas Aquinas thought, for, divorced from our seeing, there is no field of vision. We realize now the profound truth of the statement made in the first section of this chapter: our expression has a preconscious dimension. It would be out of the question to claim that the visualization of reality is a conscious and willed activity, at least with respect to its beginning. The visualization takes place through me, of course, but not as a conscious subject. It occurs on the level of what Merleau-Ponty calls the "body-subject."[6] As an intentional subject, the body visualizes, "sonorizes" and tactilizes reality, i.e., it constitutes reality as a visual, sonorous, tactile field, etc. There occurs here an expressive activity which is so profound that it runs its course on the preconscious level: we are expressive there without knowing that we are expressive. For this reason we spoke above about "hidden forms of expression." These expressive activities develop as the body itself develops; hence we do not know to what extent a newborn baby sees. Perhaps the baby's body is still so undeveloped that there is at most a capacity and a primitive inception of visualization.

Although the visualization of reality at first does not begin in a conscious way, it is continued later in a conscious fashion. Above we spoke of the visualization which occurs through the structuring of our field of vision,[7] and

[6] See Kwant, *The Phenomenological Philosophy of Merleau-Ponty*, Duquesne University Press, 1963, Chapter One "Merleau-Ponty's Fundamental Discovery: the Body-subject."

[7] Driving a car, for example, demands a very special structuralization of the visual field, and this structuralization must be learned. See the author's article "Het steeds veranderende bestaansveld van de automobilist," *De Kern, Elseviers Maandblad*, July, 1965, pp. 6–13.

this structuring is something which we accomplish partly in a conscious way: we have to learn how to structure reality. In other words, the visualization which begins on a preconscious level is continued on the conscious level. Visualization is never finished, for we can always learn to see better, to visualize the world in a better way or in a new way.

Because of the fact that man becomes conscious of his structuralizing activities, the term "expression" acquires a new and hitherto unsuspected meaning. As a rule, we do not think of expression when we devote our attention to "ordinary" seeing, listening, smelling and tasting. We usually look at such activities as the gathering of data that are already there. In reality, however, man himself constitutes the world into a field of colors, sounds, odors and flavors. Man does this as a preconscious subject, although it is true that this preconscious activity is continued on a conscious level.

It should begin to be evident now that the entire world appearing to us is constituted through expressive activity. Things and persons, for example, have a sexual meaning because we stand in the world as sexual beings. Man and woman have a mutual sexual meaning, a sexual power of attraction. There is no question here of purely subjective impressions: reality itself has for us a sexual meaning. It has this meaning through us, but, again, not through us as conscious subjects. This example is particularly useful because we are dealing here with a field of meaning which, at least in its developed form, manifests itself only later in life, that is, when man becomes sexually mature. At that age things and persons acquire a new meaning for us, without a conscious initiative on our part. Boy and girl become meaningful to one another in a way they were not before. They develop then into sexual beings, which is a form of human intentionality, and through this development reality acquires a new meaning for them. In this way values also arise: we begin to appreciate reality and through the development of our appreciation reality is constituted as a field of values. Similarly, through the development of our scientific methods, in the broad sense, the world is constituted a field of thought. Without the attitude of physical science, the world would not have become a field of physical thought.

In short, there is no appearing reality, no reality that appears to us, which we do not constitute through our expressive activity. But this statement can be understood only if we do not incorrectly conceive expression solely as a conscious activity. The objection could be raised that we assign a very unusual sense to the term "expression." It must be granted that this term is usually conceived in a much narrower sense. The reason, however, is that the expressive character of many human activities escapes attention. Who, for example, realizes that the visual field is constituted through man's visualization? We simply take the result of our expressive activity for granted and pay no attention to our own activity in this matter.[8] Once, however, we recognize our constituting activity, we cannot escape from referring to it as expressive. This term appears even more appropriate if we keep in mind that also in its generally accepted sense expression has a preconscious dimension. For this reason we referred to this preconscious dimension of expression in the usual sense before we pointed out that even activities which are not usually considered expressive also have an expressive character.

We used above the terms "receiving" and "giving" meaning. It should be evident now how intimately these two are interwoven. Our seeing is a receiving of meaning, for we appropriate, as it were, the world as a visual field.

[8] Husserl calls this the "natural attitude."

But this reception of meaning takes place through our constituting the world as our visual field, in other words, through the giving of meaning. The receiving and the giving of meaning cannot be divorced from each other. As a general truth we may say: things become meaning-for-us, they begin to exist for us, to form part of our field of existence, thanks to our meaning-giving activity. Differently expressed, we cannot enrich ourselves through impressions, except through our expressive activity. One cannot renounce all giving of meaning, all expressive activity, in order to limit himself to the reception of meaning, to the acquisition of impressions. For the giving of meaning, expressive activity plays a role in the receiving of meaning, the acquisition of impressions. More will be said about this matter in the second chapter.

3. THE OBJECT OF EXPRESSION

Man, we usually say, expresses *himself*. Even if someone is not explicitly talking about himself, we say that he expresses *himself* rather well or not well at all. "Himself" functions here as the object, but another object can be added to the verb; for example, we can say that he expresses himself very well *about* this or that particular object. Expression appears to have a double object: in the act of expression we always give expression to ourselves also, even if our expression is concerned with other matters than ourselves. In case we are explicitly concerned with ourselves, our expression has ourselves twice as its object: we express ourselves about ourselves. Because of the ambiguity involved in this double object, we will reserve here the term "object" for that *about* which one expresses himself and use "co-object" for the "self" of expressing oneself. In keeping with this terminology, we are sometimes object of our expression, namely, when we speak explicitly about ourselves, but we are always the co-object of our expression. No matter what we express, we always express also ourselves.

The object appears to be more important than the co-object of expression, for he who expresses himself, fully concentrates on the object. It is possible, of course, that someone will pretend to give expression to an object while in reality he is interested only in the co-object. But such a procedure is experienced as unnatural, because the object of expression is thus made into a means for self-expression.

Man can make everything the object of expression. In principle there are no limits to our power to speak of reality. There exist, of course, actual limits, but the latter are continually shifting. In speech and science expression assumes the form of verbalization, in painting it is visualization, in music it is "sonorization," and in dance man gives expression to realty in the rhythmic movements of his body. Even God enters into man's expression, for religious expression claims to give expression to God and His action. All this brings to mind Merleau-Ponty's statement that man is both strictly particular and strictly universal:[9] the man who expresses himself is a particular being, but from his particularity he extends himself to everything. Everything which is finds in man an expression of itself. Man is interested in everything, in the sense that he can be "with" everything and thus make it important.

In the preceding pages we occasionally used the term "to appropriate." This term is not altogether wrong, for man takes the other-than-himself up into his own sphere of existence. On the other hand, the term is not very fortu-

[9] "My life appears to me absolutely individual and absolutely universal." *Sens et non-sens*, Paris, 1948, p. 188. The pagination of this book differs in its subsequent reprints.

nate, for it makes one think of an attitude by which I place myself in the center: my property serves me. This self-centeredness is not implied when man appropriates reality through expression, for he is then concerned with reality itself and wishes to do justice to it. He intends to let reality appear and bring it to light. He has the feeling of being at the service of reality, as if reality were waiting for man in order to be brought to light. In this service, man can become tired, sacrifice his peace, live a difficult life, harm his own health. It is as if man, as the servant of reality, has the task of giving expression to reality. If the term "humanism" is supposed to convey that man must always and everywhere stand in the center, this term does not indicate what happens in man when he gives expression to reality.[10]

Man is not destined to be centered on himself, but is an intentional being. Prior to making any conscious decision, he already visualizes reality and finds himself as a being that is fascinated by the other-than-himself. When he consciously takes charge of his expressive life, he again lets himself be fascinated by the other-than-himself, by reality. When nothing fascinates us any longer, we are bored, for we fail to be fascinated by ourselves. In the following chapter, we will attempt to penetrate into the background of these remarkable facts by basing ourselves on some of Merleau-Ponty's penetrating statements.

[10] "My plan 1) the visible, 2) nature, 3) the logos, must be presented without any compromise with humanism. . . . *The visible* must be described as something which realizes itself across man but which is not at all something anthropological (therefore, against Feuerbach-Marx, 1844)" Merleau-Ponty, *Le visible et l'invisible*, p. 328. Merleau-Ponty wrote these words a few weeks before his death. While many philosophers present their views under the fashionable title of humanism, Merleau-Ponty partially wished to avoid this for reasons that will become clear later.

Reality finds its expression in man, but only on condition that man become a self. On the other hand, man becomes a self by giving expression to the other-than-himself. By visualizing reality, man becomes a subject who sees; by speaking of reality he becomes one who knows; by attaching value to reality he becomes an evaluating being. The expression of the other-than-ourselves implies our becoming as selves. This stands to reason if, with phenomenological philosophy, we accept that man is an intentional being. Man's being is a referring to, a "making appear" of the other. Man is not first something and only subsequently refers to the other-than-himself; on the contrary, his very being is related, intentional. Man is a self, of course, but this self consists precisely in the way he refers to the other-than-self. At a certain level of his existence man consciously takes up his relation, his orientation to the other-than-self. We should not think, however, that the self exists before this orientation: the self exists in this orientation and is formed through the development of this orientation. Man would not be a self-project if he could not actively take up his orientation to the other-than-himself.[11]

For this reason the expression of the other-than-self is always also self-expression: man gives form to himself by expressing the other. He discloses himself by disclosing the other-than-self. If we listen to a speaker who rises above the average, one who really brings light and opens up unsuspected horizons, he discloses reality to us and we are absorbed in the matter which he discloses. But after his speech we heartily applaud him, for the speaker could not have given us light without drawing attention to himself. We admire him. In his ingenious expression of the other-than-self he revealed a self which we admire. The

[11] This view of Merleau-Ponty implies, of course, a dynamic concept of the person. We will return to this point later.

speaker was not at all centered on himself; otherwise he could not have given us as much light as he did. Man's self-coming-to-be apparently is accomplished without his being centered on it.

Man's self-growth, then, is best fostered by not paying too much explicit attention to it. One who concentrates on his self-growth actually hampers it. In this sense it is an alarming phenomenon when there is a flood of publications and speeches about self-growth. This assertion is not a cheap moralistic statement but based on what man is. Man is an intentional being, destined to be interested in the other-than-self and to become himself in and through this interest, and not through centering on himself. In the following chapter this point will be developed more explicitly.

Meanwhile it should be evident that the phenomenon of expression occupies an important place in our life. Human existence *is* expression. The purpose of this chapter was to make sure that our point of departure would not be too narrow an idea of expression. After exploring the breadth of this concept, we must now try to penetrate into its depth.

CHAPTER TWO

Expression as the Creative Disclosure of Being

1. PHILOSOPHY AS AN EDIFICE

THE TITLE of this chapter may appear strange, and we will begin just as strangely with a note which Merleau-Ponty probably wrote in June, 1959. This note was not destined for publication, but for his own personal use. It was written in a terse style, so that a free translation appears desirable. The note is as follows:

Philosophy has a creative character precisely because it is "Being which speaks in us about itself," the self-expression of wordless experience. It is a creation which is, at the same time, re-integration of Being. For, philosophy is not creative in the sense that it builds an arbitrary edifice, one like those of which history offers so many examples. Philosophy knows itself as an edifice of words, and wishes to surpass itself as an edifice; it wishes to rediscover its own origin. It is, therefore, a creation in a radical sense, a creation which, at the same time, is an adequation, the only way ever to arrive at an adequation.

This idea gives a much greater depth to Souriau's view that philosophy is the highest art. For art and philosophy *together* are not arbitrary constructions in the universe of the spirit, of culture, but they are, precisely as creations, contact with Being. Being is *that which demands creation of us* in order that we may have experience of it. In this sense I must also analyze literature, as Being which *writes in us* about itself.[1] To most readers these words will be very puzzling. As a matter of fact, the note is very condensed and, in addition, can be understood only within the context of the whole book from which it has been taken. Those who do not understand it should re-read this text after they have studied the present chapter. We placed the text at the beginning of this chapter because the entire chapter is inspired by it and may in part be considered as its explanation. In our opinion, this text contains a kind of metaphysic of expression which is of the greatest importance for the understanding of man's expressive life. The metaphysical character of this chapter expresses itself also in its title.

Let us begin by drawing attention to a strange fact. A philosophical study is an edifice, a construction of words

[1] *Le visible et l'invisible*, pp. 250 f. The original text is as follows: "La philosophie, précisement comme 'Être parlant en nous', expression de l'expérience muette par soi, est création. Création qui est en même temps réintégration de l'Être: car elle n'est pas création au sens de l'un des *Gebilde* quelconques que l'histoire fabrique: elle se sait *Gebilde* et veut se dépasser comme *pur Gebilde*, retrouver son origine. Elle est donc création dans un sens radical: création qui en même temps est adéquation, la seule manière d'obtenir une adéquation.

Ceci approfondit considérablement les vues de Souriau sur la philosophie comme art suprême: car l'art et la philosophie *ensemble* sont justement, non pas fabrications arbitraires dans l'univers 'spirituel' (de la 'culture'), mais contact avec l'Être, justement en tant que créations. L'Être est *ce qui exige de nous création* pour que nous en ayons l'expérience.

Faire analyse de la littérature dans ce sens: comme *inscription* de l'Être."

and sentences, and this edifice is constructed by man. If someone is an original philosopher and does not merely repeat what others have said, his construction of words must be called creative. In this sense, Merleau-Ponty says that philosophy is an "edifice," a "creation." But this edifice of words claims to express that which is (*l'Être*); it would not be philosophy if it did not make this fundamental claim. Philosophy, then, is an edifice of words, which has the intention of being an "adequation," i.e., an expression of that which is, a re-integration of Being. The edifice of words is the disclosure of Being.

It stands to reason that this applies not only to philosophy but also to any form of human speech which wishes to disclose reality, as is the case with all sciences. Any scientific study is an edifice of words and, insofar as it is original, it may be called a creation. Such a human creation intends to bring that which *is* to light. Reality becomes a light for us thanks to the edifice of human words. The objectivity of science is a much-discussed problem, about which there is no unanimity. At the same time, however, it is certain that one deprives science of its very essence if one claims that science cannot possibly bring reality to light. Merleau-Ponty assigns to philosophy the privilege of knowing itself as "edifice"—he uses the German term *Gebilde*[2]—and of wishing to surpass itself as "edifice." He probably meant that, unlike, e.g., mathematics to which, as mathematics, it does not belong to reflect upon its own essence, philosophy reflects upon itself. One who asks the reflective question what mathematics is, pursues no longer mathematics but philosophy. But if the philosopher asks what philosophy is, he remains in phi-

---

[2] His notes contain many German terms, which is a sign that in the last years of his life he made a serious study of German thinkers, particularly, Husserl and Heidegger.

losophy. The philosopher constructs not only an edifice of words, but also realizes that he does this and reflects upon the function of the verbal edifice. He recognizes that Being discloses itself in it and for this reason he wishes to look beyond the edifice of words.

Merleau-Ponty applies the same view to art. He looks upon art as an edifice, a creation, through which man makes reality be a light. The painter visualizes reality, that is, he gives expression in lines and colors to that which is. The sculptor and the poet do the same, each in his own way. Art is not at all the expression of purely subjective feelings. The artist speaks of both himself and his world as an unbreakable whole. We will not attempt to justify Merleau-Ponty's standpoint in this matter here by discussing the difficult problem of art's subjectivity or objectivity.[3]

In the above-quoted text Merleau-Ponty uses an expression which at first may seem rather strange: "Being which speaks in us about itself."[4] One would be inclined to think that this is a metaphorical expression and, as such, something that the philosopher should avoid, for it is we who think about Being; hence it is not right to say that Being thinks and speaks. Merleau-Ponty, however, would reject such an interpretation: he really means what he says. He wishes to convey that Being verbalizes itself in us, visualizes itself in us, etc. We will try to explain more closely what he intends, not so much in order to present a textual exegesis of Merleau-Ponty's thought than because of the valuable vision of expressive life which, in our

[3] For a more extensive discussion of Merleau-Ponty's view and his analysis of painting see the author's *De Stemmen der Stilte*, Brand, Hilversum, 1966.

[4] He capitalizes the term "Being," as he usually does in his last work, without being entirely consistent. As the book progresses, the capitalization becomes more frequent.

opinion, is implied in his thought. The following section may seem to be removed from concern with the above-quoted text, but that is mere appearance: in reality it serves to make that text intelligible.

2. SEEING AS THE ACTUALIZATION OF THE VISIBLE

Merleau-Ponty develops the ideas which make the above-quoted text intelligible in the main chapter of *The Visible and the Invisible*.[5] He begins with an analysis of seeing and touching to show that seeing and touching belong to visible and tangible reality.[6] We can only see something really well, he argues, when our look is at the right distance with respect to the thing to be seen. This distance varies, of course, according to what we are looking at. Optimal seeing occurs at the optimal distance. Secondly, seeing would be entirely impossible without the mobility of our eyes. We know this from everyday experience; moreover, experiments have shown that genuine seeing disappears when both the head and the eyes are made wholly immobile. These two facts show that seeing belongs to visible reality. For only that which itself belongs to worldly reality can be at a distance and move itself. There are other facts that point to the same conclusion. For example, we would not be able to see someone looking if the look did not belong to visible reality.

Merleau-Ponty, then, does not accept Sartre's view that seeing is "Nothingness" (*Néant*), i.e., that it is wholly other than visible Being (*Être*). True, he does not entirely reject the Sartrian concept of "nihilation," for he admits

[5] This chapter is entitled *L'entrelacs, le chiasme*. For an extensive study of Merleau-Ponty's last work, see the author's *From Phenomenology to Metaphysics. An Inquiry into the Last Period of Merleau-Ponty's Philosophical Life*, Duquesne University Press, 1966.

[6] *Le visible et l'invisible*, pp. 172–178.

that the seer separates himself in a certain sense from the visible. (We will see later how Merleau-Ponty understands this.) But, according to him, when we speak of "nihilating" Being, this implies not only that the "nihilation" has Being as its object but also that the "nihilation" takes place in Being. In other words, Being is not only the object but also the subject of the "nihilation": the latter occurs *with respect to* Being and *in* Being. While "nihilating," that which "nihilates" does not cease to belong to Being. It is not a coincidence that in a long chapter Merleau-Ponty subjects Sartre's two absolute concepts of Being and Nothingness to a sharp critique.[7]

No matter how true it is that in our seeing a certain "nihilation" is present, this seeing continues to belong to visible reality. The case of touching is even more evident. If we wish to grasp an object, our grip must be adapted to the thing to be grasped. This adaptation is usually not attained at once. At first we often try to grasp a thing in an unsuitable way, but gradually, or after a few failures, we adapt the grip of our hand to the object. Reflective reason usually does not preside over this adaptation. A baby who does not yet have any reflections manages to adapt his grip; adults, too, usually do it without paying attention to it or even realizing that they are doing it. The adaptation of the grasping hand to the object to be grasped, then, occurs within the grasping itself. Now, it is evident that we would not be able to adapt our grasping hand, while grasping, to the object if in our grasping, our touching, we did not feel our feeling. We feel in such a

---

[7] This chapter is entitled *Interrogation et dialectique*, pp. 75–141. It is one of the sharpest analyses of Sartre known to the author. Strange as it may seem, Merleau-Ponty refers solely to Sartre's book *Being and Nothingness* and not to his *Critique de la raison dialectique*. Yet, the chapter is concerned with dialectics.

way that in our feeling we feel our feeling. This formula may sound complicated but the matter itself is simple.

In our feeling we would not be able to feel our feeling if the feeling hand did not belong to the touchable world. Following Husserl, Merleau-Ponty points out that with our right hand we can touch our touching left hand.[8] When we give someone a hand, we feel ourselves as touching and, at the same time, as touched. Merleau-Ponty, however, adds that, no matter how much we touch our touching hand, to touch and to be touched, to feel and to be felt do never fully coincide. We never reach our touching hand exactly in its touching. Granted that in our feeling we feel our feeling, this feeling and the feeling that we feel never coincide exactly. Here lies the truth of Sartre's "Nothingness." Thanks to this "Nothingness" there is a subject. There exists a blind spot and, thanks to this blind spot, there is something which we may call consciousness.[9]

Does this remark of Merleau-Ponty cast doubt on his previous observations? Must we not say that he who sees, precisely as seeing, and he who touches, precisely as touching, are not visible and touchable? The answer has already been indicated above: Merleau-Ponty wishes to

---

[8] Husserl, *Ideen zu einer reinen Phänomenologie und phäno-menologischen Philosophie*, Zweites Buch, Nijhoff, The Hague, 1952, pp. 144–147.

[9] "La négativité qui habite le toucher (et que je ne dois pas minimaliser: c'est elle qui fait que le corps n'est pas fait empi-rique, qu'il a signification ontologique), l'intouchable du toucher, l'invisible de la vision, l'inconscient de la conscience (son *punc-tum caecum* central, cette cécité qui la fait conscience, i.e. saisie indirecte et *renversée* de toutes choses), c'est *l'autre coté* ou *l'en-vers* (ou l'autre dimensionnalité) de l'Être sensible; on ne peut dire qu'il *y* soit, quoiqu'il y ait assurement des points où il *n'est pas*—Il y est d'une présence par investissement dans une autre dimensionnalité, d'une présence de 'double fond' ". *Le visible èt l'invisible*, pp. 308 f.

point out that "nihilation," precisely as "nihilation" of Being, exists not only because it has Being as its object but also and especially because it occurs only in Being.[10] This is the reason why in his book and, in particular, in his notes he so often uses the expression "the other side." He calls the soul "the other side of the body." The "nihilating" aspect is essentially only a partial aspect, for it postulates an aspect of Being. Without this aspect of Being, the "nihilating" aspect cannot exist. Being becomes a subject because it obtains a "nihilating" aspect. The fact that both aspects belong together is indicated by Merleau-Ponty in metaphorical language: they belong together as the two sides of a sheet of paper, as the two parts of a circular circuit.[11] We will return to this point later.

Seeing, then, belongs to the visible, and touching to the touchable. Seeing and touching are forms of "nihilation," but this "nihilation" takes place in the visible and the touchable themselves and remain essentially connected with them. This is the sense of the constantly recurring expression "I belong to it" (*J'en suis*). As seeing and as touching, I continue to belong to visible and touchable reality. I who see and who touch would not be able to see and touch if I were not permeated with visible and touchable reality: the latter, then, exists both outside myself and within myself. Merleau-Ponty calls this "the flesh of the world" (*la chair du monde*): this "flesh" is present as a binding element in me and the other-than-me.

What happens when a body begins to see and to touch? A visible or touchable part of reality, says Merleau-Ponty, becomes a body that sees or touches. There occurs a twofold dualization. First, a visible or touchable part of reality separates itself, as seeing or as touching, from the rest of visible or touchable reality. That which sees and

[10] *Le visible et l'invisible*, pp. 290 f. (Note of Feb., 1960).
[11] *Le visible et l'invisible*, p. 182.

39

touches is reality which sees and touches, while the environment does not see and touch. That which sees and touches is a subject, the environment is an object, but both these terms should still be taken in a weak sense here. Secondly, as we saw, in the one who sees and touches a distinction is made between the "nihilating" aspect, which is entirely proper to the seer and toucher, and the aspect of Being which he continues to share with everything visible and touchable. These two dualizations are indissolubly connected. That which sees and touches would not be a subject confronted with surrounding objects if it did not have, in addition to the aspect of Being, also a "nihilating" aspect. The body has objects outside itself because it itself acquires a kind of interiority.

Merleau-Ponty himself does not use the term "dualization" but "bifurcation"[12] and other terms, although "dualization" aptly expresses his intention. This could give rise to the suspicion that he relapses into a kind of dualism. There is no reason to fear this, however, for the aspect of Being and the "nihilating" aspect belong together as the "two sides of a sheet of paper"; both subject and object are permeated with the same "flesh of the world."

By the fact that a body begins to see and touch, says Merleau-Ponty, this body becomes the actualization of the visibility and touchability of everything.[13] By this fact the world, including, of course, the one who sees and touches himself, becomes a visual field and a field of tangible

[12] *Ibid.*, p. 180.

[13] "Il y a vision, toucher, quand un certain visible, un certain tangible, se retourne sur tout le visible, tout le tangible dont il fait partie, ou quand soudain il s'en trouve *entouré*, ou quand, entre lui et eux, et par leur commerce, se forme une Visibilité, un Tangible en soi, qui n'appartiennent en propre ni au corps comme fait ni au monde comme fait". *Le visible et l'invisible*, p. 183.

qualities. Seeing and touching are really actualizations: the visual field and the field of tangible qualities would not exist as such without the one who sees and touches. The world contains within itself the possibility to appear, and this possibility is actualized by the fact that a body begins to see and to touch. One could speak here of a self-actualization of the world brought about in the world as a whole, but then in and through the little part of the world which begins to see and to touch. It is not entirely correct to say that I who see or I who touch bring about this self-actualization of the world, for the "I," as "I," as subject, is constituted precisely through this self-actualization. There is question of a subject only by virtue of the fact that the world's visibility is realized in me. Strictly speaking, it is not right to say that this realization comes about in me, for this expression implies that I am already "there." The coming to be of the "I," of the subject is precisely accomplished in this self-actualization of the world. It is for this reason that Merleau-Ponty uses such expressions as Being sees in me, touches in me; because these things happen, there arises something like an "I," a subject. On this level of thinking it is almost inevitable that one has recourse to inaccurate expressions: Merleau-Ponty's language continues to be groping[14] and the author of this little book does not fare better.

It should be evident that the problem Merleau-Ponty discusses here is very old: it is the problem of the relationship between "Being" and "consciousness." There exists a strange paradox in this matter. On the one hand, it is obvious that we can speak about Being only insofar as

[14] "Le corps nous unit directement aux choses par sa propre ontogenèse, en soudant l'une à l'autre les deux ébauches dont il est fait, ses deux lèvres: la masse sensible qu'il est et la masse du sensible où il naît par ségrégation". *op. cit.*, p. 179.

Being appears to a consciousness. On the other, it is equally obvious that consciousness belongs to Being, is permeated with Being. It has always been a problem how a being is possible that is consciousness of Being. How can that which itself is part of reality be consciousness of that reality? Can we say that Merleau-Ponty's observations throw some light on this age-old problem? He opposes the viewpoint of Sartre, who claims that consciousness must be "nothing" in the order of Being if consciousness is to be consciousness of Being. We should not claim, says Sartre, that consciousness is something, no matter what, we should not even say that consciousness *is*. Merleau-Ponty, as we saw, rejects this view. He does not approach the problem through a reflection upon man's intellectual knowledge, but begins with a consideration of perception. This is as could be expected from the author of *Phenomenology of Perception*. He draws attention to the fundamental forms of perceptive life, viz., seeing and touching. A philosophical reflection upon these intentional activities teaches him that we need not be surprised to discover that that which sees and that which touches belong to Being. For the analysis shows that seeing and touching would be wholly incomprehensible if that which sees and that which touches did not belong to Being. At the same time, Merleau-Ponty points out that a certain consciousness is already implied *in* seeing and *in* touching. It would be wrong to say that a reflection upon seeing and touching fails to raise the problem of consciousness on the ground that consciousness lies "behind" seeing and touching. On the contrary, seeing and touching themselves are permeated with consciousness; otherwise, in its grasping, the grasping hand could not adapt itself to the object to be grasped.

For this reason Merleau-Ponty uses the term "consciousness" in the plural and speaks of "*petites subjectiv-*

ités," little modes of being a subject.[15] Let us explain what he means. While I am reflecting upon this difficult matter, I feel with my back the back of my chair, I feel my feet in my shoes, I still taste the coffee I drank a few minutes ago, and have various other similar conscious sensations. They are, as it were, spread out over my whole body. Not everything which I call consciousness disappears entirely when I fall asleep: I still chase away the mosquito that keeps pestering me, react to sounds in my dreams, hear my alarm clock, and assume a different position when my body needs it. My consciousness is not an absolute center where everything is reported, but my whole existence is permeated with consciousness.

I am not merely consciousness of myself. In my seeing the visible world becomes conscious of itself; in my touching the tangible becomes self-conscious. I am a "fragment" of Being—this expression is too materialistic, of course—in which Being becomes conscious of itself. Seeing does not occur because there is an "I," but an "I," a subject comes to be because there is seeing. The fact that a part of visible reality begins to see implies the coming to be of a subject, a becoming-"I" of Being. The subject does not stand opposite Being, but arises out of Being by segregating itself as Being-which-sees from the Being-that-does-not-see.[16] Seeing and touching, as we saw, also imply that Being is constituted a visual and tangible field. These fields are constituted from Being by the one who sees or touches.

Merleau-Ponty is not surprised that I, a particular being, can see and touch everything, for I am the self-actualization of everything visible and everything tangible. Likewise, it is not surprising that I and the others see the

---

[15] *Op. cit.*, p. 186.
[16] "C'est bien d'un paradoxe de l'Être, non d'un paradoxe de l'homme qu'il s'agit ici". *op cit.*, p. 180.

same. Some thinkers have wondered about this question, they have even asked whether it is true and, if so, how we can prove it. As a matter of fact, if the starting point of my reflection lies in my own field of existence, my own "I," if I take the subjective field as my absolute starting point, how can I ever prove that the others experience the same as I? Merleau-Ponty, however, refuses to make such a separate "I" the starting point of his reflection. For him the "I" arises precisely from the self-actualization of the visible; hence it is not surprising that the same visible reality actualizes itself in other subjects: because the same visible reality actualizes itself in all seeing subjects, all see the same. Merleau-Ponty, therefore, sees no real problem in the intersubjectivity of seeing and touching.

Through seeing and touching, we saw, Being is made visible and tangible; in the one who sees and touches, Being is thus made accessible to itself. This accessibility *originates* together with and through seeing and touching. There is no previously existing accessibility, hampered by obstacles, and for this reason such terms as "unconcealing" and "disclosing" can be confusing. They suggest that accessible Being lies hidden behind a veil or a cover and that making Being accessible consists in removing the cover. No, Being becomes accessible through seeing and touching. It does not become accessible for something outside Being but for itself in the one who sees and touches, for they belong to Being. Merleau-Ponty does not deny that a physiological preparation is needed for this purpose: there is no seeing without the eye, no feeling without a nervous system. Merleau-Ponty says but little about this physiological preparation: he merely mentions that it should not be considered the *cause* of seeing or touching. His view can be compared with that of Henri Bergson's *Creative Evolution*, to whom he often refers in his later works.

It is hardly subject to doubt that Merleau-Ponty wished to apply the view derived from his analysis of seeing and touching to all levels of human existence and that, e.g., he also wanted to understand abstract thinking in this fashion.[17] True, in his explicit statements he leaves the question open whether abstract thinking should be understood in this way. In our opinion, however, he does this merely for reasons of methodic prudence. He died before he could finish his latest work and had intended to discuss strictly intellectual life in the later chapters. For this reason, he did not wish to mention the conclusions of the later chapters in the earlier ones. But in his notes he constantly used such expressions as Being thinks in us, Being speaks in us: in other words, he does not hesitate to apply to man's intellectual activities expressions derived from his analysis of seeing and touching.

Moreover, he emphasizes that even so-called pure ideality—that of abstract ideas—is not without a body; here also there is question of the body and "its other side," the soul. He even goes so far as to wonder whether seeing itself is already incipient thought;[18] if the answer is affirmative, then developing thought must, of course, be understood in line with incipient thought. In a penetrating passage, he compares so-called "fleshy ideas" and "pure ideas."[19] By "fleshy ideas" he means ideas whose ideality is indissolubly connected with matter, as is, e.g., the case with a melody, a painting or dancing. There is really question of ideality here, for a melody can make a deep and long-lasting impression on us, a painting can speak eloquently to us, and a dance can have a profound spiritual meaning. The "fleshy idea" gives us the happy conviction that material reality in us and outside us is not

---

[17] *Op. cit.*, p. 180, p. 200.
[18] *Op. cit.*, p. 191.
[19] *Op. cit.*, pp. 195–200.

deprived of depth. Now, the "fleshy idea" has in many respects a greater power than the abstract idea. With respect to the latter we say that we possess it, but with respect to the former we should rather say that it possesses us. Once we have acquired an abstract idea, we go on; usually we do not dwell with it. A "fleshy idea," on the other hand, can, as we saw, occupy us for a long time; a melody, for example, can haunt us for days. Once someone has learned to savor the ideality of "fleshy ideas" he will not easily think that he can overcome this ideality. In other words, is not all ideality "the other side" of the body? Is there really any other kind of ideality? These reflections show the direction taken by Merleau-Ponty's thought, even though he wished to leave certain questions unanswered until he could discuss them *ex professo*. Unfortunately, as we saw, death took him before he could do this.

3. CREATION AND ADEQUATION

After this long digression, let us now return to the text of Merleau-Ponty quoted at the beginning of this chapter. He calls there philosophy a creative activity and records the strange fact that in and through an edifice of words we arrive at knowledge of Being. Philosophy is an "edifice," it knows itself as such, nonetheless, it is "re-integration of Being." He then formulates a general statement which seems to be most important, viz., Being is that which demands creation of us in order that we may have experience of it.

Before considering why this statement is so important, let us first pay attention to a terminological question: we would like to replace the term "creation" by the broader term "constitution." Merleau-Ponty speaks in this text about art and philosophy, both of which lie on the level of man's conscious and free existence. This conscious and free existence, however, takes up man's preconscious and "pre-free" existence, according to the viewpoint which Merleau-Ponty developed in his earlier works and which he continues to hold here, as is evident from his analyses of seeing and touching. Now, the term "creation" can be used only on the level of man's conscious and free existence. But Merleau-Ponty's statement, that Being demands creation of us in order that we may have experience of it, applies not only to the conscious and free level of existence but to every level, provided we replace the term "creation" by a more general term that can be used also with respect to the preconscious and "pre-free" level of life. Such a term is "constitution."

Constitution occurs on all levels of our intentional life, and in the sphere of freedom and consciousness it assumes the form of creation. Thus, we can read Merleau-Ponty's statement in this form: Being demands active constitution on our part in order that we may have experience of it (Being). The experience of Being, then, we owe to our constituting activity: we must constitute Being as a field of experience in order to be able to experience Being.

The same idea has already been expressed in a different way: the giving of meaning is necessary in order that there may be a receiving of meaning. Through our meaning-giving activity Being becomes meaning for us. Now, constitution, the giving of meaning has an expressive character: we make be something that was not yet there. For this reason there is an unbreakable bond between expression and adequation.

It is not easy to indicate exactly what Merleau-Ponty means by the term "adequation." One of the traditional definitions of truth, as the "adequation of intellect and thing," probably played a role in his choice of this term. The Latin *adaequatio* is composed of the particle *ad*, which indicates direction toward, and the adjective *ae-quus*, level or equal. Thus the term implies a movement to equality. It was used to refer to a fundamental movement of experience, of knowledge: in his knowing, man wishes to reach that which is, he wants his knowledge to be a rendition of what reality is, and to the extent that he reaches this goal his knowledge is true. Merleau-Ponty must have had this in mind when he selected the term "adequation." The term, then, has a pregnant sense, which the reader should keep in mind when he studies Merleau-Ponty.

At first, it may seem that there is opposition between expression and adequation. Expression implies that we make be that which is not yet. It seems that by expression we move away from that which is and enter creatively in the empty space of what is not yet. Adequation, on the other hand, is a movement toward that which is. Now, the thesis of Merleau-Ponty is that adequation occurs only by virtue of constituting, meaning-giving expressive activity. This important thesis is the topic of this chapter.

With Merleau-Ponty, we emphasized the important point that this thesis applies also to the basic forms of our experience, viz., perception, seeing and touching. It was precisely through the analysis of these elementary forms of experience that Merleau-Ponty was led to formulate his thesis. Seeing and touching arise because a piece of visible and tangible reality becomes the realization, the actualization of the entire visible and tangible field. There is, we saw, no subject which precedes seeing and touching and brings about seeing and touching, but the birth of seeing and touching from visible and tangible reality is precisely the actualization, the realization of the subject. This constitution, this expression is both reality's coming to be accessible and the subject's coming to be a subject.

The same applies to all expression. At first we are

inclined to take a rather superficial view of expression. We think that the subject himself and his experience of reality are prior to expression: the subject, we assume, must exist and must have experience of reality through all kinds of impression before he can give expression. This "obvious" view now shows itself very superficial; it fails to do justice to the fundamental role which expression plays in man's life.

Expression does not follow adequation, but it is through expression that adequation takes place. Verbal expression, for instance, is not an activity that is consequent upon a pre-given adequation, but in the verbal expression there occurs a new adequation with reality. Our speaking is not the expression of a pre-existing light but the birth of light. This birth of light takes place through us, but not in us, at least not in the strict sense of the term, for it is reality itself that becomes a light. We should not be misled by the fact that, as experience shows clearly, there is something in us which precedes our speaking. When we manage to express something, the situation is not that, before speaking, we did not know the matter at all, while subsequently we knew it. The fact that we knew something about it prior to our speaking does not mean that the light which is given expression in our speech was already present before we spoke, but indicates that our speaking is also partly based on preverbal modes of expression. Through our speaking, however, reality becomes a light for us in a new way. (It goes without saying that speaking is understood here in the broadest sense of the term and does not merely refer to speaking with other persons.)

In the same perspective Merleau-Ponty considers also painting.[20] He refers to a painting as "something visible in

[20] *L'oeil et l'esprit*, Gallimard, Paris, 1964.

the second power," to indicate that the painting is a visualization of reality which presupposes and is the expression of another visualization. We must make a distinction between the first visualization occurring in our seeing and the second, which takes place through the act of painting. Merleau-Ponty refuses, however, to divorce these two visualizations. Although seeing is something common to all men—except the blind—there exists in different people a great difference in level of seeing, of visualizing reality. There are gifted people who see on a high level: they alone can make good photographs, produce a good television show, make a movie or paint. Both the first and the second visualization of reality have the character of a constitution-adequation. By seeing we constitute reality as a visual field; by painting we constitute a visual picture which, as it were, embodies the essence of a visual reality on canvas. The visual picture on the canvas is not a faithful copy of visual reality, for why would an artist make a copy of an original that is right there before his eyes? The painted canvas is a constitution-adequation through which we receive a new vision of reality.

Work also has the character of a constitution-adequation. Marx describes work as human self-expression.[21] He accuses capitalism of robbing the working man of the fruit of his labor, his self-expression in the world, in exchange for a bit of money. According to Marx, it is in this that the worker's "essential alienation" consists, even if he is paid well. Man's self-expression in work, however, is at the same time adequation, for work is the appropriation, the making accessible of the world. By expressing himself in the world, man makes the world his field of existence. His labor gives rise to a world with which he is familiar. With respect to work, also, it is true that "Being demands

[21] "Zur Kritik der Nationalökonomie," *Kleine ökonomische Schriften*, Dietz Verlag, Berlin, 1955, p. 135.

creation of us in order that we may have experience of it." For in and through work, man acquires experience of Being in a very special way. A skilled craftsman is familiar with his materials and means of labor in a way that cannot be fully expressed in words. That is why man needs to work, even with his hands. Now that mechanization and automation increasingly make manual labor unnecessary as a means to earn a living, this form of work returns as a leisure time pursuit, a hobby, destined to become increasingly more popular.

Playing also is a contribution-adequation. Through play the body and the world acquire for man a meaning which they do not have outside the sphere of play. One who does not at all, or only barely, know how to play is blind to an entire dimension of reality. A child which has no opportunity to play often fails to grow up to fully mature adulthood. The meaning in question arises through play and is accessible only in terms of play. The non-playing man—if there is such a being—simply does not understand the field of existence, the world of the playing man. It is not easy to reflectively express the meaning of the field of play in words. Let us add that man often also plays with words, but it is also difficult to say in what this playing with words consists.

The constitution-adequation is also, as should be evident from the preceding considerations, human self-realization. There exists no finished subject prior to the expression. If man expresses himself in a new way, he thereby gives a new form to his own existence. The renewal of expression is a renewal of existence. Sometimes this renewal is superficial, but it can also penetrate deeply into human existence. For instance, when modern technology arose, man learned to express himself through his work in the world in a new way; a striking characteristic of this new mode of expression is its social nature. Many imposing results of modern work could arise only through collaboration. The new mode of expression very profoundly influences human existence. By adopting this mode of self-expression, modern man became a new type of man, without even noticing it. But there are also superficial phenomena of fashion which imply merely an ephemeral change of expression and of our mode of existence.

The constitution-adequation is not limited to the intellectual and technical realms. We do not merely visualize reality, make it tangible and express it in words but also value it. This valuation does not occur through an intellectual reflection upon values, for such a reflection presupposes their existence. Again, it is not easy to say how, by valuation, we constitute reality as a value. Sometimes, we accomplish it by a respectful common form of behavior, which is also a form of expression. For example, judicial proceedings are surrounded with a certain solemnity: the judge is robed, the hall of justice is more or less imposing, and the language used is solemn. All this helps to constitute the value called "the law," which in this way is raised above ordinary everyday life. Similarly, we accentuate the social value of marriage by a certain solemnity and by a festive celebration. If we strip values of their luster, it can easily happen that they will not survive. On the other hand, we surround new emerging values with such a luster because, without our expression, reality would not become a value for us. Nevertheless, it remains true that we are very badly informed about the expression which constitutes reality as a value.

The constitution-adequation is a phenomenon occurring in very many forms. We gave a few examples above, but did so only in a superficial way. Each of them would really require a profound study. How do we constitute reality as a value? Which meaning of reality is revealed by man's playful self-expression? Which dimension of reality is disclosed by work? How do we constitute the value of our fellowman by our respectful behavior? How do we bring the mysterious reality of God to light through cultic expression? Merleau-Ponty's proposed scheme could be illustrated only in a more or less abstract fashion here, for only a specialist in each of the dimensions illustrated by the examples could adequately develop them.

Merleau-Ponty's idea about the constitution-adequation is particularly useful to make us aware of the many ways in which man is disclosure of Being. Every form of expression has the character of a disclosure of Being, opens our eyes to a particular aspect of reality. It can happen, of course, that a particular form of expression is not exactly very revealing; after all, no phenomenon of human life is always genuine. There are books and articles about scientific topics which manage to say nothing; paintings that do not speak to us; music which holds no power of appeal; ways of playing that are not really playful. It would be foolish to think that everything which presents itself as expression is authentic and really has the character of a constitution-adequation. Not everything presenting itself as expression is really expressive; there is much expression empty of content. Half-failed expressions often precede the genuinely successful expression. Expression alway intends to be adequation, but is far from always being successful, and if it does not succeed, it is not expression in the full sense of the term.

Moreover, as we noted above, not every expression is adequation in the same sense. One form of expression can have a more striking character of adequation than another, and there is much diversity of form in expression and adequation. It can happen that the one is more open to this form of constitution-adequation, and the other to that form. There are people, for example, for whom a philosophical study holds no appeal, and others to whom music means nothing. Human existence has many registers, and it is not given to everyone to play all of them.

If, however, the expression is authentic, it is always a disclosure, an unveiling of reality. The reason why has been pointed out in this chapter: expressive life has a metaphysical dimension, and this dimension is present in the whole of man's expressive life.[22] But only the philosopher becomes conscious of this dimension and points it out. It is proper to all expression to be a constitution-adequation, but only the philosopher recognizes it as such. It is his task to penetrate into the grounds of expressive life.

This chapter is a commentary on one important passage of Merleau-Ponty's last work, a commentary given in the spirit of that entire work. Although this book is not meant to be an historical study of Merleau-Ponty but a thematic work, the best way to throw light on the theme, so it seemed, was to develop the topic in Merleau-Ponty's spirit. In the following chapters, we will examine some of the implications contained in his fundamental idea.

[22] "On le verrait au contraire si l'on comprenait que peindre, dessiner, ce n'est pas produire quelque chose de rien, que le tracé, la touche du pinceau, et l'oeuvre visible ne sont que la trace d'un mouvement total de Parole, qui va à l'Être entier et que ce mouvement embrasse aussi bien l'expression par les traits que l'expression par les couleurs, aussi bien *mon* expression que celle des peintres". *Le visible et l'invisible*, p. 265.

CHAPTER THREE

Expression and Interiority

1. A THINGLIKE CONCEPTION OF INTERIORITY

TURNING against a one-sided interpretation of reality, a philosopher is sometimes tempted to express himself too forcefully. This happened to Merleau-Ponty when in his Preface to *Phenomenology of Perception* he wrote: "There is no inner man."[1] For centuries, philosophers and men of science, spiritual writers and literateurs have spoken of man's interiority, they have discussed the value of an interior life and said that no man can be fully human if he is wholly absorbed in external things. It is simply impossible to imagine that all these people spoke merely about a fancied reality, about nothing real. Merleau-Ponty combated a certain conception of man's interiority. He had a good right to do that, but not, of course, the right to reject interiority as such in the process. Actually, in spite of the above-quoted words, he does not really reject all interiority, but only a certain interpretation of it. We, too, have done the same in the preceding pages, e.g., when we said that what is given expression by man does not pre-exist in his interiority as a finished reality. To describe expression in a responsible way, however, it is necessary to clarify interiority, for the very term "expression" indi-

[1] Humanities Press, 1962, p. XI.

55

cates an outward movement, a movement whose starting point lies in the interior. Thus the question must be considered of what is meant by interiority.

As we pointed out, one who begins to reflect upon knowledge is inclined to give a naively realistic interpretation to man's cognitive field. He does not at once notice that by seeing we visualize reality and, therefore, conceives the visual field as a pre-given reality which we appropriate by looking at it. Man tends to such an interpretation with respect to all knowledge and not only insofar as sense knowledge is concerned. If this naively realistic interpretation were right, we would find outside ourselves a finished cognitive field, which we merely need to make progressively our own. Let us add that insufficient attention has been paid to the fact that with respect to man also we are inclined to such a realistic interpretation.

The human psyche also is a field of inquiry. Aristotle wrote not only about nature but also about the soul, in particular about the human soul. In our universities there are courses not only about physical science but also about psychology. Now, just as nature was conceived as a finished reality, so also sometimes the human soul was presented as if it were a ready-made datum which one could progressively make one's own. True, the human soul was a reality of a different type than nature outside man. While nature was open to external observation, the psyche was accessible only through introspection. Man is a conscious living being, and this implies that in all his experiences he co-experiences also himself. Through his experiences, he knows what seeing, hearing, sensing, thinking, loving, etc. are. In this way a distinction was made between the inner world and the outer world, and as long as people thought in a primitively realistic fashion, both were conceived as given realities.

Dualism was born from this primitive realism: there

are two orders of reality, the external reality of the world and the internal reality of the soul or mind. As is well-known, the distinction between these two orders assumed its sharpest form in the philosophy of Descartes, who reduced the external reality of the world to extension and motion and, consequently, everything else to soul or mind. Yet, although this dualism received its sharpest form in Descartes, he certainly was not its originator.

One who adheres to this dualistic standpoint and conceives both the external and the internal as realities, albeit of different orders, cannot escape conceiving expression as a movement which originates in the order of internal reality and moves toward that of external reality. Expression then is the passage from interiority to exteriority. In this view one will readily arrive at the conclusion that what is given expression leads a double existence: first it exists in man's interiority, and then it has an exteriorized existence, an existence in matter, in the world. Our thinking, for example, is an interior reality and has its exteriorization in the word, in speech. Similarly, the artist possesses in his interior an idea of the work to be made; he then reworks matter according to this idea, so that the latter also acquires an exteriorized existence.

In this hypothesis it is not easy to discover what possible sense expression could have for the one who expresses himself. For he has his internal thought, and this thought is finished. Why, then, should he give also an exteriorized existence to this same thought? Thought itself does not need this external duplication, from which it can gain nothing. The only possible sense of exteriorization would be that it serve the purpose of communication. By exteriorizing our thoughts, we can make others familiar with them and become acquainted with theirs: there can be a fruitful exchange of ideas. This is perhaps the reason why in the past so much emphasis was laid upon language as a means of communication: there was a tendency to see the entire essence and meaning of language in communication.

Those who accepted this hypothesis experienced great difficulty in assigning a place to sense experience. Thinking and free decisions obviously belonged to man's interiority, but where did seeing and hearing take place? Some viewed them as activities of exteriority, of the body, others, such as Augustine and Descartes, held that they were activities of man's interiority, of his soul. The latter, however, got into difficulties with the seeing and hearing of animals. If they admitted that animals see and hear, they were forced to ascribe a soul, an interiority to animals; if they refused to do this, as Descartes, they had to deny that animals see or hear in the strict sense of the term.

Traces of dualistic thought continue to exist, especially in all kinds of linguistic expressions, but one can no longer say that scientific thought is dominated by it. Introspection is no longer the actual method of psychology, which now proceeds rather through observation and experiment. This method presupposes that the core of what man is does not consist in an interiority, which is altogether beyond observation. The fundamental data of psychoanalysis do not fit in with dualism; yet psychoanalysis has solidly established itself in scientific life. Similarly, the linguistic sciences presuppose that thinking and speaking are interwoven in such a way that it is no longer possible to make a dualistic separation between them. Thirdly, those who *ex professo* are occupied with man's expressive life know that man needs expression in order to become himself; this point is particularly emphasized in modern pedagogy and didactics. Finally, the theory of evolution, which is no longer a mere hypothesis, is difficult to reconcile with the dualistic standpoint. True, the question whether or not man should be conceived in a dualistic way properly belongs to the realm of philosophy. But in man's pursuit of science an implicit philosophy is always at work, and the implicit philosophy which dominates today's science is certainly no longer dualistic. In other words, our objection to a dualistic interpretation of expression aimed at a past that has already largely been overcome.

Whether one thinks dualistically or not, however, man's interiority cannot be rejected. Terms like "man's inner life" retain meaning. The initiative for many expressive activities arises in man's interiority. But what is this interiority? To what extent is expression really a movement from within to without?

2. INTERIORITY AS THE "OTHER SIDE" OF THE BODY

With respect to these questions Merleau-Ponty's last book indicates the road to a solution. As was pointed out in the preceding chapter, the intentional dualization established a certain separation between subject and object: it is precisely for this reason that one can speak of dualization. "I belong to it," says Merleau-Ponty. One who sees essentially belongs to visible reality. The man who sees and what he sees both are permeated with the same "flesh of the world." The same substance of worldly reality is present in the man who sees and the external object seen by him. A distinction, nonetheless, is made, for man is the one who comes to see, and this cannot be affirmed of the things that are seen. When his seeing has become a fact, man finds himself as a subject surrounded by objects. This subject is not entirely concealed from himself. Although reflective consciousness is not yet present in sense perception, the latter is not entirely unconscious. Otherwise, as we saw, seeing and touching would be wholly impossible: we could not feel, touch, in a way adapted to the object if in our feeling itself we did not feel our feeling; we would then be unable to adapt our touching hand to that which we are going to touch. If for this accessibility to ourselves a term is needed, we must use "consciousness," but there is not yet question here of a reflective consciousness. There is merely a beginning of consciousness which is present in the perceiving body. One could not even speak here, says Merleau-Ponty, of a consciousness that is numerically one, for this kind of consciousness is spread over the whole body. For this reason he uses, as we saw, the term "consciousness" in the plural.

In the spirit of Merleau-Ponty we referred to seeing and feeling as expressive activities, for reality is visualized and made tangible. Seeing and feeling essentially refer to the world, but they also imply a certain consciousness and, consequently, the constituting of a self, a subject. The body cannot see or touch without becoming accessible to itself. If one wishes to speak of a "soul" here—as Aristotle did—we may say with Merleau-Ponty that this soul is "the other side" of the body.[2] This soul is the inner side of the externally perceiving body, and without this inner side perception itself would be impossible. Soul and body belong together, says Merleau-Ponty, as the two sides of a sheet of paper, as the two sides of a circular circuit. What he means is that the soul is not a heterogeneous reality with respect to the body and that the body could not be a body without that inner side, the soul. This inner side is constituted when the body begins to see and to touch, the body's turning to without necessarily implies the constitution of the inner side. The body constitutes itself as a perceiving body and as having an inner side in one and the same development: these two aspects cannot be divorced

[2] This expression occurs very often in the notes constituting the final part of his latest work.

from each other. This kind of turning to without is at the same time interiorization. The term "interiorization" is aptly chosen because it expresses that interiority comes to be, that the body constitutes itself as interiority. It is in this sense that we will use the term "interiorization." It is important that from the start we realize that the body's turning to the world and interiorization do not remain opposites in this view.

Thus, the hypothesis can be made that the development of man's intentional turning to the world, its rising to a higher level, implies also a progressive interiorization. This hypothesis is in line with what we saw in the preceding chapter, viz., that the development of intentionality is an increasing dualization. According as man, as "movement of transcendence," brings about in himself higher forms of turning to the world, he becomes more "subject" and reality outside him becomes more "object." This coming-to-be of the subject is an increasing interiorization. The coming-to-be of the subject and that of the object are the two sides of one and the same medal.

This idea can be found in several contemporary thinkers. Sartre, for example, very often uses the term "interiorization" in his *Critique de la raison dialectique:* he refers to man as "interiorization" of the field of existence, the world. Man realizes his dominium over the world through interiorization. Sartre does not mean that the world is taken up into a pre-existing interiority, for he does not admit such an interiority: man is nothing but a "project" orientated to the world. For Sartre, interiorization is a turning to without, to the world, a turning which experiences itself as such, controls itself in freedom, directs itself. It is, we could say, an outward movement having an interiority. By virtue of the fact that there is this interiority, there is an "I," and because there is an "I," there exists a being which can make the other-than-itself its own.

Sartre and Merleau-Ponty agree that interiority and turning to without are essentially connected. If we think away man's orientation to without, his "existence," his intentionality, nothing remains. But this turning to without would be purely thinglike and, therefore, not human if it did not have an inner side. The more interior, the more human also it is. On the other hand, there is also an important difference between Sartre and Merleau-Ponty. According to Sartre, perfect interiority, i.e., consciousness and freedom, was present from the very beginning of man's unfolding of his human existence. He began with absolute and sovereign freedom, but in the course of history his freedom has become incrustated with unfreedom and his interiority has lost its purity. This lost freedom must be regained. From the preceding pages, it should be evident that this Sartrian idea is foreign to Merleau-Ponty.

In Emmanuel Levinas also we find a view which in many respects agrees with that of Merleau-Ponty, although these two philosophers are markedly different in their approach. The second part of Levinas' book *Totality and Infinity*, which has the subtitle "Interiority and Economy," describes the rise of consciousness. Levinas does not, of course, wish to be an historian who assigns a date to the rise of consciousness; he merely tries to discover an intelligible line in the coming-to-be of consciousness. Now, according to him also, consciousness's coming-to-be is an interiorization which runs its course in man's turning to the outside. Levinas sees enjoyment as the most original relationship between man and the world, and this enjoyment implies, in spite of all compenetration with the world, a beginning interiority. He who enjoys is pleased and experiences himself as such. Man arrives at a higher form of consciousness when through work he renders his existence secure. He then begins to live in a dwelling and thereby also constitutes an "external world" which for him begins to have the character of an object. At the same time, he develops his objective thinking, which assumes the character of a bid for power. It is beyond the scope of this book to reproduce the whole of Levinas' impressive view. The important point for us is to see that in his view also interiorization and turning to the world are indissolubly united.

Accordingly, the hypothesis that the development of our turning to the world and our interiorization go hand in hand can be found in several thinkers. But what indications are there for the truth of this hypothesis? Here we may appeal to experience. It often happens to men that they are internally renewed when they turn in a new way to the world. There often is a striking change in children when they reach school age. They are forced to begin to exist in a new way, together with other children, in a classroom, under a new kind of discipline, different from that at home, devoting their time to a fixed program of learning. Within this new way of turning to the world, the child's interiority also changes. Similarly, a striking change occurs when education is over and the young people become involved in a task in today's world of work. This change in the external situation brings about changes also in their interior life. The philosopher himself observes something similar in his life. When he decides to become acquainted with a trend of thought that was hitherto unknown to him, he attends certain lectures or reads books which previously he disregarded, in other words, he turns in a new way to the world. At first, he simply becomes merely acquainted with a new terminology and new ideas. Later, he feels at home in them: he begins to follow the lectures or authors, as it were, from within and is able to anticipate what has not yet been said. He can read books about that trend of thought in a critical fashion, i.e., he sees when they take a wrong turn. That is not all, however. Sooner or later he will discover that he himself has begun to think differently. One cannot become familiar with a valuable trend of thought without undergoing an interior renewal.

Moreover, it can happen that changes occur in our thought without our initiative or even without our being aware of the fact that these changes are taking place. A thinker who for several years has paid no attention to a particular topic and then returns to it often notices that he no longer faces that problem in the same way. It is possible, then, to change one's view about a topic without even reflecting upon it. This can happen because we exist in a world, a common world, and in this world many changes take place, whether we notice them or not. These changes affect us also, they go "through us," and they penetrate into our interiority.

It can happen that the members of a group, in particular, of a closed group, have an established and fixed way of speaking about themselves, society and their common values. It can happen that this way of speaking is protected by a kind of common censorship—which need not be the formally institutionalized type. It can happen, however, that such a group and its members undergo a change but continue to use the fixed categories of speaking about themselves. Communists, for example, keep talking about themselves in a certain way although they have become different; the same happens to members of religious orders who live a secluded life. Thus, even the fact that one continues to speak of oneself in the same way does not mean that the inner man remains the same when changes occur in his worldly situation.

Even though we are conscious and free, then, we do not have full control over the changes occurring in us. For this reason man rightly asks himself what it will mean for him that he initiates a new way of dealing with the world.

Man has introduced technology, for example, and has thereby become the technical man. By devoting himself to a different external *praxis*, he has become innerly different. We are innerly different also because we now move around in the world in different and faster ways. Similarly, we are innerly different because we have become a race of city dwellers. Every new form of existence in the world implies an inner difference in man. In this sense we may say with Merleau-Ponty that the soul is "the other side of the body."

All this, however, does not imply determinism, for we ourselves take the initiative in changing our situation. And when we take such an initiative, we indirectly also take the initiative to change ourselves. We cannot change our situation without also changing ourselves. For this reason modern man wonders what it means that he is now entering an era of automation, he wonders what cybernetics will mean for him. Such initiatives are directly concerned with exteriority, the external field of existence, but indirectly and inescapably they are also concerned with man himself. All this applies not only to the macrofield of existence, the larger aspects of life, but also to the microfield. One who gets married, for example, takes the initiative to coexist with a fellowman: by doing this, he or she will also become innerly different.

The parallelism between turning to the world and development toward interiority can also be observed in the growth of the individual man. The little child in his crib has a very restricted field of existence: he provides for his needs by drawing attention to himself, he sleeps and plays with his body and with objects placed close to him. One can hardly speak of an inner life here. When he is a little older, he begins to reconnoiter a broader world and then there occurs an increasing interiorization: the parents notice that the child has a will of his own and that he begins to understand situations. When he begins to talk, he first imitates sounds without making the meaning of words his own, but as soon as he begins to speak, in the proper sense, he also begins to think. During the age of puberty there arises a new relationship to the world and his relation to other persons becomes different: there occurs then a new form of interiorization, which can sometimes disturb the previous equilibrium. A special science, genetic psychology, describes how the development of relationships with the world goes hand in hand with increasing interiorization.

We wish to emphasize once more that man's turning to the world and his interiorization are *mutually* dependent.[3] Arguing against the hypothesis of an absolute interiority, one that is divorced from our turning to the world, we wish to put the accent on the fact that interiority is bound up with our turning to the world. The reverse, however, is also true: our turning to the world can be renewed only if our interiority renews itself.

But what is our interiority? Interiority is not, as we saw, a world apart, existing in its own secluded and encapsulated way, distinct from the external world. Interiority is man's being with himself, but a being-with-himself which is accomplished in his being-with-the world. For man is "existence," and all activities which he finds in himself are intentional activities. But, one could object, are there not words which indicate what happens "in" us without any reference to the world, such as knowing, loving, being bored or lonely? In reply, we must say that all such words refer to intentional activities, and the latter

[3] "All this implies that a sharp dichotomy between internal and external, between language that is 'intransitive,' i.e., not directed to the communication of information, and 'transitive' language is impossible." C. A. van Peursen, *Feiten, waarden, gebeurtenissen*, Meulenhoff, Amsterdam, 1965, p. 16.

imply a correlate; or they indicate our disposition, which always refers to a situation. No matter how deeply we penetrate into ourselves, Merleau-Ponty points out in his *Phenomenology of Perception*, we always find there the world. It appears to be very difficult to describe our interiority: our thinking is attuned to the world and we are used to demarcate a particular reality from the rest if we wish to make a description of it. We localize, as it were, our object by distinguishing it from that which does not occupy our attention. In the same way we would want to demarcate our interiority before describing it. Our interiority, however, is not a datum that stands side by side with other data, but is an aspect of our existence. And the latter also is, strictly speaking, not a reality which stands side by side with other realities.

Of course, one can always assume an objectifying attitude and say, e.g., that side by side with rocks, plants and animals there exists also a being called "man." But before we can assume such an objectifying attitude, we experience our being-man as that through which everything else is accessible. Our objectifying attitude is borne by this more primordial experience. Man is not a worldless look falling on the world and distinguishing rocks, plants, animals and men in it. On the contrary, man is an intentional reality for which and through which everything appears. Even when I objectify and place rocks, plants, animals and men before my objectifying look, I must make a distinction between the objectified man and the objectifying man: the former is obviously dependent upon the latter. The objectifying man is not "just another one" among the appearing phenomena, but is the one to whom everything else appears. I cannot help experiencing myself as a center, and whatever appears, appears to and through this center. I do not experience myself in the first instance as a part of reality but as the one for whom and through whom there is such a thing as the whole of reality. I know, of course, that I am not absolute but, in spite of it, whatever is accessible to me is only accessible as appearing to the relative man I am. I am, as Merleau-Ponty says, wholly particular, but in my particularity I am, at the same time, wholly universal because from my particularity I extend myself to everything.

I am "with" the world but, at the same time, I am also "with" myself. My being with myself and my being with the world constitute an unbreakable whole.[4] If I begin to be with things in a new way, I also begin to be in a new way with myself, and vice versa. I co-experience my interiority in all my experiences, but I do not have a separate experience of my interiority. I am unable to silence my experience of the world in order to limit myself to the experience of my interiority. True, in an objectifying attitude I can speak of my interiority alone, for in objectifying thought practically everything can be isolated. But we are then dealing with an abstraction and not with an isolated experience of my interiority.

All this does not imply that the co-experience of my interiority is of less value that the experience of the so-called external world. For, if I did not co-experience my interiority in all my experiences, there could be no question of an "external world." The only reason why we can speak of an external world is that we always co-experience our interiority.

We develop our own life of experience, as is readily evident from the fact that the term "to know" today has a

---

[4] " 'L'autre coté' veut dire que le corps, en tant qu'il a cet autre coté, n'est pas descriptible en termes *objectifs*, en termes d'en soi,—que cet autre coté est vraiment l'autre coté *du corps*, *déborde* en lui (*ueberschreiten*), empiète sur lui, est caché en lui,— et en même temps a besoin de lui, se termine en lui, s'ancre en lui. Il y a un corps de l'esprit, et un esprit du corps et un chiasme entre eux." *Le visible et l'invisible*, p. 313.

sense which it did not have one thousand years ago. Our knowing has become different because there exist now physical sciences and many other kind of empirical sciences. "To know" will again acquire new shades of meaning when in the future new sciences come to flourish. We should not think here of "materially" supplementing gaps in our knowledge, for in that case it is possible to add to our knowledge without modifying what we know already. But when man develops new ways of knowing, the existing ways also are affected. The philosopher experiences this very clearly. Two thousand years ago philosophy was already in existence, but the pursuit of it has changed since the rise of the empirical sciences. One can no longer pursue metaphysics in the same way as it used to be done. When man develops his cognitive life, the world becomes a cognitive field in a different way, but his own interiority also develops differently. Our interiority changes when we begin to occupy ourselves with the world in a new way. Human interiority is not a datum that perdures unchanged in the course of centuries. If Plato were reincarnated in our time, he could no longer write his dialogues. Too much has changed in our approach to the world and, therefore, also in our interiority, than that a contemporary could still write as Plato did.

Perhaps it would be better not to use the noun "interiority" but to speak in its stead of "aspect of interiority." Our existence has a twofold aspect: an aspect of turning to the world and an aspect of interiority; these two are unbreakably united and develop together. Teilhard de Chardin wrote about the increase and development of interiority, and in this sense he wrote about interiorization. It was not a coincidence that he wrote about this in an era when man, more than ever before, appropriates the world to himself. The growth of our bonds with the world is bound to be accompanied by the development of a more-encompassing interiorization. Merleau-Ponty's concept of dualization implies the same: the development of human existence always means that both the object-aspect and the subject-aspect develop together.

If this is so, then it is altogether impossible to describe expression in terms of bringing something from man's sphere of interiority to that of exteriority. If the aspects of interiority and of exteriority are unbreakably united in their origin, then all fundamental forms of expression will always be expression of both the world and our interiority; then we are unable to express the world without co-expressing ourselves, nor able to express ourselves without co-expressing the situation in which we are interwoven. It is not to be excluded that one sometimes may wish to speak only about himself. It can only be done, however, after assuming an objectifying attitude and thus making an artificial division, existing only in the sphere of abstraction, between two aspects which of themselves are connected. In such a case we try to think analytically, which is something made possible by objectifying abstraction. But if then we wish to see to it that our speaking is not uprooted, in other words, if we wish to speak of concrete reality, we will notice that, in speaking of ourselves, we always also give expression to our situation, our world.

Expressive life is the realization of the bond with the world in which man attains existence, it is always a disclosure of man and of the world. This formulation, however, is not without danger. One could interpret it as if man always further develops his bonds with the world. Such an interpretation would be one-sided, for man also dwells in the bond with the world which he has already realized. Man constantly repeats the forms of expression that have already been established. Work, for example, is self-expression in the world, but numerous men work the same way day after day. The table is laid in the same way and the meal put on it is familiar to us. We listen to music we have often heard before and go through familiar steps in dancing. People converse without intending to arrive at new truths. It would be bad if the whole of life were orientated toward the preparation of the future, for man would then become entirely restless.

In our time the dynamic attitude is more prevalent in the West than it used to be in the past or is in some other parts of the world. Yet, even we have not forgotten how to "dwell" in what we have or are. We live in the present but are borne by the past. It would be bad for us if every "today" were to make quickly way for "tomorrow." We remain attached to forms of expression that have already been realized and do not let them be pushed aside too easily. Man cannot always be creative, one can even say that he is only creative at exceptional moments of his life. Our life is not only a being on the way toward meaning but also a dwelling in meaning. We do this, for example, when we spend a few pleasant hours with friends, and our home is, of course, emimently the place where we "dwell." Our culture is the result of expressive activity on the part of our ancestors right down to long-forgotten ages. We do not wish simply to abandon this heritage, even though we live in a more dynamic era. We "dwell" in an established meaning also when we celebrate a feast: we then leave the creative efforts to those who organize it, but we ourselves are content to celebrate it.

To conclude this chapter, let us say a few words about the *ex* of "expression." Although expression is not a kind of "translation" from man's interiority into the external world, the particle *ex* is meaningful: through his expressive life man makes forms of meaning arise from a soil that remains always fruitful. He actualizes something that was present in capacity, in accordance with the Aristotelian theory of potency and act, which holds that the act is the realization of possibilities contained in potency. Expressive life is an outward movement, not one that starts from man's interiority, but from the interaction between man and world, which is a kind of ever fertile capacity. In the actualization of this interaction the initiative comes from man, no matter how much man's possibilities are given to him by the world. In this sense one can say that expression is something which comes from man.

The objection could be raised that there exist forms of expressive life to which all this does not apply. When, for example, someone writes a novel, his book, so it seems, expresses something that does not at all exist in reality: it is a pure product of his imagination. It is true, of course, that a novel is not a scientific treatise and does not intend to express objective reality: the persons who people the novel are imaginary persons. But they also are placed in a situation, a relationship to equally imaginary fellowmen. Even though the imaginary world depicted by the novelist does not express real life, that world is connected with real life. In the real field of existence, there are always reasons why the novelist writes as he actually does. His book can applaud the real conditions of life—usually such a work is not very forceful—or it can be an indictment of real life. The novelist cannot even depict a fictitious situation which has nothing to do with the real situation. Even if he does not write a novel with a bias, his attitude toward an existing situation will exercise influence on his writing. For this reason novels, in particular great novels, always exercise a certain influence—enough to make the censors of dictatorial regimes block their publication or oppose their widespread dissemination. The novelist, then, also shares in his own way in the development of the common situation. His influence can sometimes even be greater than that of scholarly publications because he speaks a language that can be understood by many people.

A different question is whether religious expression falls under the above-given description of expressive life. We will postpone this question until the last chapter.

Chapter Four

Expression and Playfulness

1. The Difficulty of Defining the Playful Element

THE FACT that there is a playful element in expression can be observed even in children who still lie in the cradle and whose expressive life merely begins to develop. The child plays with his own body and with the little things placed near him. His movements are useful also, for it is only by moving in this way that his bodily organism can properly develop. If all movement were made impossible for the child, he would die. But his necessary and useful movements are performed in a playful way. The child is easily induced to play, and even his feeding can be changed into a game. Children who do not wish to eat often change their mind if a game is made of it. For grown-ups also a task that can be performed playfully is more easily done. Annoying chores can be made more attractive by introducing an element of playful competition. The element of play, then, is present from the start in human expression. Let us add that it is not limited to human expression alone:[1] the playful gambling of little lambs in a meadow is one of the most-beloved spring

[1] Cf. F. Buytendijk, *Het spel van mens en dier*, Kosmos, Amsterdam, 1932.

scenes. The sexual life of animals also can sometimes display a very striking element of playfulness.

It is very difficult to define the playful dimension of man. To define is to indicate the limits, but the playful element is something whose limits are not easily found.[2] Playfulness reveals or can reveal itself in every form of expressive life. One could ask, would it not be possible to arrive at a definition by starting with an analysis of those activities which can be referred to as play without any qualification? Parents, for example, will tell their children that it is time to stop playing and begin to study; in other words, we make a distinction between playing and not playing. Unfortunately, activities that are said to be play are very often not performed in a playful way, they can to a large extent lose their playful character. Television sometimes brings us a football game played by highly paid professionals, but can their activities be said to be "play"? When a purse of $10,000 or more depends on a single stroke of a golf club, can we say that the masterful stroke so successfully executed by a champion is playful? With respect to children also one can often notice that their playing does not always run its course playfully: romping often degenerates into a fight. It can happen that a boy who is not very playful when he plays discloses more playfulness during his study hours. The playful element reveals itself in all forms of expression, but hardly ever in a perfectly pure form; no expressive activity is entirely playful. Accordingly, although each one knows from experience what is meant by playfulness, it is very difficult to define this aspect of expressive activity. The

---

[2] "Asking about the essence of playing, we are caught by the numberless variations in which playing presents itself." E. Vermeer, "Discussie over het spel en zijn betekenis voor het kind," *Persoon en wereld*, ed. by J. H. van den Berg and J. Linschoten, Bijleveld, Utrecht, 1953, p. 168.

same happens also in other matters; for instance, everyone knows what humor is, but where will one find a definition that is satisfactory in every respect?[3]

2. Play and Reason

We should realize, first of all, that playfulness does not arise from reason. Let us explain this statement. The orderly arrangement of life by reason can mean two things. Something can be arranged by reason in the sense that all of it, or nearly all of it, arises from reason itself. This happens, for instance, in mathematics. True, mathematics starts from a given point of departure, viz., our perception of extension and the fact that we can situate ourselves in extended reality with our body. One could even say that our motion in the extended world is a kind of "mathematics": we cannot throw a stone, jump across a ditch or safely cross a street without "measuring"; otherwise the stone would not reach the point aimed at, we would fall into the ditch, come into "conflict" with motorcars. We exist in the extended world and move in it in a way adapted to the situation. Mathematics, however, cannot be considered a simple continuation and development of our existing in space and measuring with our body. While the existence of mathematics is conditioned by our spatial existence and bodily measuring, reason abstracts from all this a starting point for a scientific development that is not purely expression of perceptive data. Mathematical definitions are not a faithful expression of what is given in perception but rather axioms formulated on the occasion of such data. The field of mathematical thought

[3] We have experienced how difficult it is to give a conceptual definition of humor; hence we will not even attempt one." J. Linschoten, "Over de humor," *Tijdschrift voor philosophie*, vol. 13 (1951), p. 663.

is almost entirely constituted by reason itself and therefore wholly intelligible to reason. Formal logic offers another example: it abstracts from contents and concentrates on intelligible connections of thought. Its constructions are purely rational and therefore wholly intelligible to reason. One could say that organizing reason is here almost fully autonomous: reason is fully and purely reason.

There is, however, also another way in which reason can organize life.[4] Wherever people live together, there is order and this order comes from reason. Reason, however, is not autonomous here. Common life has to be organized in such a way that there is sufficient time for sleep, work, recreation and eating; in short, the many different needs of man must be taken into account. Reason arranges things here, but it does not constitute the things to be arranged. It finds them pre-given and must understand them. It can happen that reason shows no respect for them and tries to arrange life without understanding certain human needs. If this happens, reason builds a frame of life in which man does not feel at home and against which he will revolt. Why, for instance, does a mother play with

[4] Consequently, the term "science" does not have a fully univocal sense. "Now that man realizes that, aside from causal laws, there exist also other types of law, such as statistical, structural and taxonomic laws, there is a tendency to break the connection between determination and causality and to understand the term "determination" as referring to any way in which an event is fixed by previous conditions according to any type of law. Let us add that with respect to qualitative changes or connections, such as those dealt with by philological-historical sciences—the working or influence of persons, works or ideas—the term "to determine" has never had the rigorous meaning which it should have in a strictly causal view or theory. Certain nineteenth century theories much too readily assumed such a rigorous meaning when they claimed that 'milieu or social being determines consciousness.'" K. Kuypers, "Verklaren en oorzakelijkheid," *Alg. Ned. tijdschrift v. wijsbegeerte en psychologie*, vol. 54 (1961), p. 57.

her baby when she takes care of him and feeds him? It is such a waste of time from the standpoint of rigorous efficiency and usefulness. The only possible answer is that the baby happens to need this play and the mother is happy to oblige. If reason wishes to organize baby care, it must understand this need and take it into account.

It is in this second sense that man's playing is organized by reason. Reason devises the implements of play, it creates room for it and formulates the rules. The development of play would be impossible without reason. But it is not due to reason's initiative that man is playful, that he needs to play in order to be able to live as a human being. This point should be clear from the preceding pages: even animals are playful, and little children play long before their rationality has sufficiently developed to let reason establish order in their lives. Man's playfulness, then, is something pre-given; it does not arise from reason itself. We are not playful on the basis of rational motives.

Thus it is not surprising that it is difficult to penetrate into the motives of man's playfulness by means of rational reflection. Why man is playful is a question that is just as difficult to answer as why he laughs at humorous sayings, is sometimes bored, or likes to look at beautiful things. In these and other realms life runs its course in relative independence from reflection: we understand man's motives in these matters without fathoming them by reason. It often happens that existential and rational motivations do not coincide. In our era man is intensively preoccupied with rational motivation, but it is not at all excluded that he is guided—misguided, we should say—by one-sided ideas which are inadequate with respect to his real, existential motives. Thus it can happen that certain existential motives do not occur in the world of rational motivation. Life, however, will run its course then, regardless of the rational motivation. Those who are guided by existential motives will then assume an attitude of contempt with respect to rational motivation, they will tell the intellectuals who represent rational motives in no uncertain terms what they think of them.

Let us give a few examples. The order of life established by Marxism is strongly dominated by what they call "scientific socialism." They organize life in terms of their way of scientifically reflecting on man and prescribe the real man, in terms of their reflection, what he should be.[5] But does this "scientific" order do justice to man as he really is? Does he feel at home in a Marxist order and is he willing, in the long run, to accept this order? There are several developments which indicate that the "weight" of the real man makes itself increasingly felt in the U.S.S.R. and other communist countries and that the Marxist order is being given less weight. It is not a coincidence that literary writers play an important role in this matter. While the men of science and the philosophers— these two groups work in close collaboration under Marxism—pay special attention to rational motives, the men of letters are mostly led by existential motivations. If these two groups are out of harmony, the literary writers will easily come in conflict with the ideology established on the basis of the rational approach.

Another example may be taken from this side of the "iron curtain," though there are symptoms of it also on the other side. We have established an order of life which is largely attuned to a rationalized society of work, and the education given to our young men and women is geared to this rationalized labor order. At present there is a certain

[5] The ultimate ground why Marxism has a dictatorial character must be sought, I think, in the alleged scientific character of socialism, in the light of which Marxism wishes to organize the whole of life. In this way life is compressed within the framework of a theory.

amount of opposition to such an order of life; in particular, young people take the initiative in the revolt against it. Their actions are often characterized as an irruption of the irrational manifesting itself in their music, dancing and dress. But, is it not rather a revolt against the narrow and one-sided rationality which dominates both intellectual reflection and practical life? Are not their actions inspired by repressed existential motives?

One can even ask whether it is right to speak of the motives underlying man's playfulness, in the sense that the very use of the term "motives" points too much to a rational sphere. For, one could argue, man is only genuinely led by a motive when, before he acts or does not act, he closely examines the question which of the two is better. What reasons are there to act, and what reasons not to act? There can be a responsible human choice only when a decision is made after considering all the relevant views of the matter. Such an exclusively rational sense, however, should not be attached to the term "motive."

Let us not forget that this term is derived from the Latin *movere*, to move. The motive is that which moves us to act or not to act, and it is certainly not true that man is solely moved by purely rational and carefully considered motives. Why do people light a cigarette during a conversation? Why do we try to finish one conversation and prolong another? Why are we delighted to read one book and ready to close another as quickly as possible? Why does a beautiful spring morning tend to put us in a joyful mood? Or, if one wishes to remain in the realm of the rational, why are we fascinated by a clear and forcefully presented argument? Why do we attach so much value to the light of truth? Plato was not a man who undervalued reason, yet he says that Eros moves us to seek the truth. Plato's *Symposium* has a passional overtone when he speaks of the search of truth that is started by Eros.

Our motives, then, as a rule, are not rational, in the sense that they have arisen from reason. It is true, of course, that reason can acknowledge these motives and arrange them in an orderly fashion, but in that case reason recognizes something that exists independently of itself and whose existential rhythm has not been planned by it.

If motives, however, operate independently of reason's initiative, if their operation has an existential rhythm which does not coincide with the rhythm of thought, how can our reason "catch" such motives in concepts, how can we express them in words? Obviously, this is very difficult. We have, as it were, to transpose into the registers of rational thought something which is not "at home" there: we try to express in a rational sphere something that lives outside that sphere. The contrast can be very striking, as is evident when one reads rational reflections on the sexual togetherness of married people: the attitude which a person assumes when he considers this topic rationally is very different from the attitude of a married couple in their sexual togetherness.

Accordingly, we should never forget that, if we rationally express matters that are not in themselves rational, there is a danger that the field of reason and the field of existence will be out of harmony and that our rational expression may become unfaithful to what we wish to express. Our rationalization of the field of existence can disclose a far-reaching absence of "feeling" for what reality is. This danger is not at all imaginary, for it can easily lead to a mutilation of existence, especially if certain rationalizations become generally accepted. In such a case we, together with many others, look at life through a distorting pair of spectacles and fail to recognize that they are distorting. We think that the real field of existence coincides with the distorted field visible through our spectacles, we become blind for everything that cannot be seen

81

through them and deny even that there is anything else to be seen. If on the basis of our distorted rational vision of life we then proceed to organize life, it can easily happen that important dimensions of human existence will be given short shrift. In some religious sects, for example, a certain rationalization led—and still leads—to very narrow possibilities of sexual life. Similarly, there have been educational systems which did not permit children and adolescents to be young people: they had to be "pocket editions" of mature adults. Life has sometimes been rationally ordered in such a way that the embodied character of man seemed to have been forgotten. Undoubtedly, every era—ours included—has its own narrow views restricting certain dimensions of life, without even being aware of it, for when man begins to become conscious of the fact that his view is too narrow, this narrowness is destined to disappear soon. In the long run, life is always, and fortunately so, stronger than any theory.

Let us add one remark. It is fortunate that the existential motivations often operate independently of reason's motivations. Man has not yet managed to find a satisfactory definition of humor, but fortunately he continues to laugh at jokes. Thus no danger for man's playfulness needs to be implied in the fact that we do not manage to define it satisfactorily. Danger arises only if, on the basis of inadequate or even false rational conceptions, one proceeds to organize life; for example, if on the basis of an inadequate view of playfulness, one wishes to prescribe to what extent children will be allowed to play. Planning and organizing reason must be conscious of its own inadequacy.

Contemporary philosophers, therefore, sometimes plead for an "enlarged reason."[6] By reason in the strict sense

---

[6] Particularly, existential and phenomenological philosophers, such as Binswanger, Merleau-Ponty and Dondeyne.

they then mean the human intellect insofar as it operates according to the method of rigorous conceptualization: the intellect does not scientifically affirm anything save insofar as the affirmation can be justified by the rigorous methods of logic. Reason, these philosophers argue, should realize that man's "understanding" goes beyond such narrow confines. We understand many aspects of reality, without being able to justify what we understand in a strictly rational fashion. Such an understanding can be called "extra-rational" if one wishes to reserve the term "rational" for the above-mentioned rigorous method. Enlarged reason, then, is the reason which recognizes the limitations of the rational in the strict sense and therefore admits that there is also light outside this strict sense.

There exist at present two trends of thought with respect to this matter. The first says that certain aspects of reality can *not yet* be known according to reason's rigorous methods because our rationality is not yet sufficiently developed. Meanwhile, however, we should not abandon the ideal of an all-pervading, rigorous rationality. In other words, what those philosophers call "understanding" through an "enlarged reason" is merely a primitive stage which in principle can and must be overcome. The second trend of thought, however, argues that there is no question here of any "not yet," but of a situation that exists "in principle": the domain of rigorous rationality is in principle limited, we must as a matter of principle admit that there exists understanding outside the sphere of the strictly rational. Improved scientific methods may perhaps be able to shift the limits of what is open to strictly rational understanding, but they cannot entirely abolish them.

Without trying to discuss this question here in detail, we would like to remark that the opinions about the matter cross the "party lines" of philosophical trends of thought. Husserl, the founder of phenomenology, never gave up his belief in the ideal of rigorous science, in the possibility of fathoming our field of existence by means of rigorous reason. Many phenomenologists, however, who consider themselves his followers, do not agree with him in this matter and are protagonists of enlarged reason. Wittgenstein, one of the founders of analytic philosophy, thought it possible once and for all to fix the domain of rigorous science without, however, denying that outside this domain there exists for man meaningful reality which somehow can be understood.[7] But as a philosopher and as a man of science, man must remain silent about that reality. Precisely among analytic philosophers, however, there are many today who adhere to the ideal of rigorous science and who believe that reason, if it becomes mature enough, will be able to approach everything in a rigorously scientific fashion. Personally, I am in favor of this second view, but, as was mentioned, we cannot discuss this matter here in detail.

3. CHARACTERISTICS OF PLAYFULNESS

What makes expression playful? A first requirement is that the one who expresses himself enjoys life and the world around him. We do not mean that whoever takes pleasure in something expresses himself playfully, but that he who playfully expresses himself enjoys what he is doing. One who is very thirsty can guzzle a glass of water without any playfulness, yet he visibly enjoys his drink. Let us add, however, that as a rule playfulness occurs when there is question of refined enjoyment. A special dinner is not a success unless the guests eat, drink and converse in a playful way. Similarly, the enjoyment of a

[7] *Tractatus logico-philosophicus*, 6.52 and 6.522.

good glass of wine or liquor is surrounded by playful customs. Although enjoyment can exist without playfulness, the two are closely connected. A baby who is really hungry or uncomfortable does not play, but he begins to play when he is being taken care of or lies contented in his cradle. When after a long winter in their stable, cows return to the meadow, they express their enjoyment of the new situation by a skittish playfulness that is not in keeping with their bulk. Someone who feels ill at ease can hardly converse in a playful way. One who is in a black mood until he has had his morning cup of coffee does not begin the day with playful conversation.

Emmanuel Levinas says that our most original relationship to the world is that of enjoyment.[8] The world is for our organism the place where it is at home: the world provides for our needs and fills our existence. It is light for our eyes, sound for our ears, food for our stomach, oxygen for our lungs: we experience our contact with the world as something that fills our existence. Organism and world belong so much together that our organism's enjoyment is in and of the world. The relationship of enjoyment between organism and world is pre-objective: in our enjoyment we are too interwoven with the world to let this world be an object. A meal or music which we enjoy is not an object for us, nor is the beautiful picture in which we take delight. The attitude of one who enjoys is not that of the art critic who endeavors to give an objective description. Enjoyment, nevertheless, implies a certain consciousness: if the way in which something fills our existence were totally unconscious, there could be no question of enjoyment. One can argue whether Levinas is right when he claims that enjoyment is so primordial that everything else develops from it; yet it is certain that enjoyment is an

---

[8] *Totalité et infini*, pp. 82–86.

original aspect of our existence and cannot be reduced to anything else. Now, man's playful expression belongs to the domain of enjoyment of the world and life. Thus there is no room for playfulness in religious gatherings dominated by deadly seriousness. The liturgy can only be affected by playfulness if the participants experience a kind of religious happiness, if they enjoy being together in a religious context.

Playfulness is the spontaneous expression of the fact that one enjoys the situation, there is a certain absence of concern. One who feels really in bad need cannot act playfully, a certain sense of security is needed to play. By acting in a playful way, one expresses enjoyment of life and environment: playfulness is a "yes" to life. If too much emphasis is placed on the Heideggerian "thrownness," i.e., if one thinks that it is characteristic of man to be "thrown" into a world where he finds it difficult to feel at home, playfulness becomes difficult to understand. The same applies if the Sartrian "nausea," boredom and aversion, are seen as man's fundamental situation. It is simply impossible to conceive playful man as someone who feels "thrown" into the world or whose fundamental mood is one of "nausea."

It is true, however, that playfulness is endangered by a working world in which everything is organized around the profit motive and no care is taken to arrange things in such a way that the worker can feel at home in his work. There is hardly any room for playfulness at a conveyor belt, at least in reference to the work itself. Whatever playfulness occurs there is extrinsic to the work, and it will occur only among people who have become resigned to their situation. (We abstract here from the question whether such resignation is desirable.)

It is not excluded, of course, that play can be cruel. In the past there were people who could make a game of torturing their fellowmen. Such people felt at home in a world in which fellowmen were reduced to objects of play. Such a degeneration is difficult to understand for one who does not consider his fellowmen as things. Yet, sadism is a human possibility, which can manifest itself even in children: one meets sometimes young boys who play by torturing animals. The sadist enjoys a situation of cruelty.

Another characteristic of playfulness is that it requires a sphere of freedom. Freedom, however, is a concept that is analogous in many ways; hence let us indicate in what sense the term is used here. By freedom we mean here that man does not act under compulsion, that his expression is not imposed upon him from without. To act playfully, man must be in a situation in which his expression is born from within. Playful behavior cannot be imposed, in the strict sense, from without in such a way that spontaneity is excluded. One can, of course, invite playfulness, urge someone to participate in playing, even organize a game. But it has to be done in such a way that the external invitation is innerly accepted; otherwise there is no genuine playing. If children feel that they *have to* take part, regardless of their inner acceptance, they can still go through the motions but they do not really play.

It is not excluded that an action which in a certain respect is imposed from without still leaves room for spontaneity in its execution. In that case there remains also room for playfulness. If, for example, children have to do the dishes, they may not like it at all and would not do it if they saw a way to get out of it. But given the necessity of performing that disliked chore, they still find room for playfulness. Occasionally they even manage to extend that room so much that the washing and drying of the dishes itself is improperly done.

Certain facts could be adduced that seem to contradict these considerations. One who plays can genuinely continue to play even if he submits to stringent rules. In any game that reason helps to devise there are rules; such a game cannot be played without observing the rules. Even children realize this and object to companions who do not play "fair," by excluding them the next time they wish to play. It is true that observing the rules often belongs to the very structure of playful activity, but this does not exclude that the playful activity itself remains free. This activity is, inclusive of its rules, freely accepted. One who wishes to be free of the rules can always accomplish this by not playing. By accepting to play, he accepts also from within the rules of the game.

This is also the reason why playfulness and seriousness are not opposites:[9] one can play in all seriousness and, nonetheless, authentically play. Seriousness does not conflict with the playful character of a game. Children will sometimes refuse to let someone play with them because he does not wish to play seriously; card players are notorious for the serious demands they impose upon their partners. One can also play, of course, without any rules, cavorting around in freedom according to what strikes one's fancy at any moment. A child does this when he gambols around in a meadow; likewise an adult who goes for a walk in the woods and looks at whatever attracts his interest. The dog which follows him on his walk is even more playful in this respect than his master. But, as should be evident from the foregoing, this kind of freedom is not essential for every game or play.

All this implies that "elbow room" is needed if man's playfulness is to have an opportunity to assert itself.

[9] "In our consciousness play stands as the opposite of seriousness. At first, this opposition remains just as irreducible as the very notion of play itself. On closer inspection, however, the opposition of play and seriousness appears to be neither exclusive nor fixed." J. Huizinga, *Homo ludens*, Tjeenk Willink en Zn., Haarlem, 1938, p. 8.

When everything is regulated down to the last details, playfulness is asphyxiated. The fifteen minute break that used to be given at mid-morning between classes was an absolute necessity because in class itself there was hardly any room for playfulness. Everything was carefully regulated: how to sit and hold the hands when listening, how to write by exactly imitating model letters, and how to reproduce an exact copy of a model drawing. One hardly learned to express oneself playfully. Today this is fortunately no longer the case, for it is very important that, even when a task is assigned, as much room as possible is left for playful freedom. By leaving this room for freedom, one can see to it that the task's fulfillment comes at least in part about through the initiative and the spontaneity of the child himself. In this way his self-expression is stimulated.

All this applies not only to the individual but also to the group *as* a group. A group of children can be busy without being busy as a group; for example, if they are together in a room and each one for himself tries to solve a problem of arithmetic written on the black board. But a group acts as a group when it executes an action which is structurally common. Even in such a case there can be spontaneity if there is room for someone to assume informal leadership and the group can, on its own initiative, accept this leader. The action of the group arises then in playful freedom. Undoubtedly, it is very difficult to give this kind of leadership to a group of adults; yet it is leadership in the most proper sense of the term, for in this way the group becomes a unified whole from within and not by an external imposition.

Playfulness can go together with a rigorous order, provided this order arises from within. This happens when the order originates at least in part from each one's sensitivity to the others' actions. A recent international festival of music offered eloquent illustrations of this assertion. Several bands performed freely and playfully, but in such a way that there was also a perceptible order in which each tone and each movement of every band member fitted neatly together with those of the other band members. Yet there was no rigid regimentation by a leader whom everyone had to follow blindly. Such a unity of playful acting is impossible without great sensitivity for one's fellow players. It stands to reason that this kind of spontaneous adaptation to one another can only be the result of much practice and great familiarity with each one's "playing characteristics."

Man's very thinking comes playfully into existence, even in the most rigorous sciences. To understand this, one should not pay attention to the article which the mathematician or physicist writes after his ideas have taken shape. He will write his article in accordance with the demands of rigorous logic, in such a way that each step forward is logically accounted for. But that is not the way in which his thought comes into being.[10] The decisive insight can arise at the most unexpected moment, even at a time when the premises from which the insight is to be proved are not yet clear in his mind. It can happen that no progress is made during hours of intense study and that the light suddenly dawns during a quiet walk when the mind is not even consciously occupied with the problem. Anyone who pursues scientific work knows this for a fact from his own experience. An idea, then, often is born in a playful fashion. The same can be said about inventions, as is evident from the many stories about inventors who "by chance" invented what they were vainly trying to invent by systematic research.

Playfulness implies that one enjoys his activity, that the

[10] Plato's *Dialogues* are a prototype of the playful birth of ideas.

latter can, at least to a certain extent, originate spontaneously and in freedom. For this reason playfulness requires also a certain lack of tension. One who is tense can hardly play. Being relaxed does not exclude exerting oneself: one can exert himself while playing in a relaxed way. Exertion means that one concentrates his attention and uses all the powers at his disposal, while being-tense indicates a lack of freedom and spontaneity. One who is tense acts under pressure from within or from without, he does not have the freedom needed to play. As a matter of fact, one of the means recommended to overcome tension is precisely to induce the tense person to indulge in play.

These are some of the characteristics of playfulness. No matter, however, how much playfulness may belong to an authentically human existence,[11] it is not an absolute ideal. For it is possible for man to be too playful or to be playful at the wrong moment. When we meet someone who has just suffered a bereavement, we should not converse playfully with him. The same applies to a nation just struck by a serious disaster. Children can be so playful that their studies remain fruitless. Exaggerated playfulness can also harm a nation in its work. This observation is in agreement with what was said above: playfulness is an aspect of man's expressive life. One whose expressions show hardly any trace of playfulness is an unhappy man, but on the other hand, expressive life must also reveal other aspects than playfulness. It ought to be directed to the classical ideals of truth, goodness and beauty. Truth is an ideal because in our expression we bring reality to light. In our expression we usually address ourselves to others; thus we

---

[11] "The connection between art and play has been too uncritically accepted upon the authority of Schiller's statement that man is only perfect insofar as he plays." F. Buytendijk, "Bijdrage tot de algemene psychologie van de dans," *Paedagogische Studiën*, vol. 26, no. 12, p. 12.

should respect them and treat them as fully human beings, and this belongs to the ideal of goodness. The ideal of beauty demands that our expression have an attractive form. Expression has also a utilitarian aspect, for through our expression we make the world a place where we can dwell. The playful element of expression may not jeopardize these other elements; in other words, man must play in a suitable way. It is hardly possible, however, to express this statement theoretically in more detail.

In present-day society there is a shortage of playfulness. The rigid organization of the world of work left little room for playfulness in the recent past, and the situation existing in the world of work influenced education. The average worker was viewed as someone unable to take an initiative and therefore the labor order left no room for initiative on his part. This view continues to exercise influence even today.

The lack of playfulness in our expression manifests itself also very strongly in many newly built residential sections of cities. Monotony and lack of creative imagination are the predominant feature. Although the situation is improving somewhat, it is still far from satisfactory. Utilitarian provisions are much better, of course, than they used to be, but very little seems to be done about providing for man's fundamental need for playfulness. This condition may be connected with the modern divorce between work and art. In former eras work and art were integrated, at least far more than today, now they are separated. Thus work developed as an artless pursuit, and art became something "eccentric." The building of houses must again become a real art if the residential areas are to leave room for playfulness. The builders must keep in mind that it is very difficult to live playfully in an environment that is not built in a playful way. Houses must be built with an eye for the human beings and all their fundamental needs, and this means that "enlarged reason" rather than sheer rationality should preside over the design.

There is—or was—then, a lack of playfulness in the world of work and that of dwelling, in education and training. Western man has made great progress in the utilitarian realm, but not in that of playfulness. With respect to the latter, he has not even managed to maintain the level reached in past ages. Thus it is not surprising that pleas are made now in favor of "ludic" formation, education in playfulness. This education, however, may not be limited to adding a new activity to others. True, there are activities, "games" or "plays," in which playfulness predominates, but we should be playful in all our activities. Provisionally there is no need to be afraid that Western man will become too playful; on the contrary, he is undernourished in this respect. Even our so-called games are largely deprived of playfulness. Where, for instance, is playfulness in the Olympic Games, except perhaps in the opening and closing ceremonies? Where is playfulness in a football match? Professionalism in such games may be inevitable, but it is a danger for man's playfulness.

Professionalism may be needed because people like to watch a well-played game. A good portion of the leisure hours resulting from the increased productivity of man's work are filled with watching others play, and our demands for perfection in the execution of a game continually increase. Thus the players have to devote themselves full time to the game, they become professionals. For the professional player, however, it is often difficult to play in a playful fashion, even though externally they may seem to be very playful. The playing itself often no longer matters to the professional player. The spectators, on the other hand, are passive, they do not behave in a playful way. Thus it can happen that playing reigns supreme while playfulness does not permeate concrete existence itself. We do not object to professionalism in sports, provided it does not eliminate the playful element from everyday existence. Watching others play may perhaps become an incentive to make more room for playfulness in daily life, but there is no guarantee that this will happen. The educational atmosphere in which children and adolescents grow up is likely to be a more important factor.

In speaking about playfulness, we have hitherto mentioned play or game only in an incidental fashion. Let us therefore devote a few lines to them. The playful element can predominate so much in a particular activity that we simply indicate it as "playing." Even very small children can play; perhaps we must even say that playing occurs in its purest form among them. When their needs are satisfied and they feel at peace with the world, they often begin to play. They move around simply because they like to move, and follow one another or anything that moves. They are delighted with things that make noise, they love taking things apart and putting them crudely together again. They are playfully busy and delight in their busyness. In this way they explore the world and one another. There is no question of any rigorous purposiveness in all this, but it is as if being busy with themselves, the world and one another is the very purpose of their busy-ness.

The need of children to play is obvious but can occasionally become troublesome to adults. Any parent knows how children can manage to transform the world of grown-ups into a world of play, thereby going counter to the "intentions" the adults have embodied in the things of their world. Mother does not want her china changed into playthings, and the traffic officer objects to seeing the roads transformed into a playground for boys. This is one of the reasons why of old all kinds of special things, toys, were made for children to play with: by giving them something to play with, one makes playing possible for them and prevents them from making the world of the grown-ups into a plaything. That would be dangerous also for the children; hence all kinds of games have been organized for them, games requiring a playground, implements and a certain organization of the children's activity. There is a kind of fluid transition between the spontaneous playing of children and their playing with the toys made by adults, for the latter try to make their toys fit in with the world constituted by the child, they try to channel what the children do spontaneously in such a way that the transition appears acceptable to the children. In the playing of children roles also are sometimes used, e.g., playing father or mother, doctor or nurse.

Even in children playful activity can be crossed by intentions that are no longer purely playful. The urge to be the "boss" can be very strong and make the game degenerate into a fight. Similarly, greed can reveal itself in the desire to have more or bigger marbles than the others. Many motivations familiar to us from the world of adults can disclose themselves also in the playing of children.

Adults also play a large variety of games: chess, checkers, cards, theater, games of chance and the many games in which the use of bodily forces play a decisive role. As was pointed out, many activities that are called games or plays can be performed in a way which is not at all playful. Sometimes the possibility of gaining money is used to make playing more attractive, and in this way greed can begin to have a decisive role. Is it not strange that gambling games, such as roulette, are still called a form of playing? Playfulness obviously no longer predominates when fortunes are at stake. Playing the stock market is a deadly serious business, which should be reserved for professionals. Once a person's livelihood or prosperity is involved in playing, his activity becomes work in the full sense of the term. It is then no longer possible to let playfulness predominate in that activity.

Playing, in the strict sense, implies that one does something because one likes it, and as long as one likes it, for the sake of the inner meaningfulness of the activity itself. As soon as a form of playing becomes a profession, it assumes an air of "having to" that is not always easily reconcilable with genuine playfulness. It is difficult to imagine playfulness predominating when two teams are tied in the world championship match, a few minutes before the end of the game, and the difference between winning and losing can amount to thousands of dollars for each player. When our playing becomes a paid spectacle for others, its playfulness is in jeopardy. Fortunately not every form of playing suffers from this handicap.

All this made it seem dangerous to us to devote our attention solely to so-called games in studying the playful dimension of man's self-expression. There are people who hardly ever play games and who, nonetheless, exist in a very playful way. There are others who make some form of playing their profession and who, nonetheless, do not exist very playfully. The playful dimension can express itself in plays and games but fortunately also outside them.

The preceding analysis of man's playful dimension is, of course, far from adequate. Playfulness is an important aspect of human existence, but defies adequate description because it occurs everywhere and does not permit itself to be isolated. Playing with words itself offers a rich field of inquiry. Not only the humorist plays with words, but almost everyone, including the university professor who lectures on a very serious topic. We play with words when we converse at table or drink a glass of beer with friends.

Playfulness occurs also in religious expression—witness some of the rainspouts in medival cathedrals, the exuberance of certain liturgies, the atmosphere of religious ceremonies in Italy or Spain. All this indicates that our analysis of playfulness remained very inadequate. Yet, something had to be said about it in this study of man's expressive life.

CHAPTER FIVE

Verbal Expression

1. SPEECH AS ADEQUATION WITH BEING

IN THE preceding chapters we spoke of expressive life in
general, even when our attention was directed to playfulness. While playfulness undoubtedly is only one aspect of
man's expressive life, it remains true that playfulness is
something that can reveal itself in all forms of expression.
In the present chapter we will consider one particular
form of expression, viz., verbal expression.

It is necessary to indicate more accurately in what respect verbal expression or language will be considered
here, for language is a very broad and complex topic.
There exist many sciences devoted to research in matters
of language, and philosophy also is intensively occupied
with it. Even one who wishes to study language philo-
sophically can approach the phenomenon of language
solely from a restricted standpoint.[1] Here, then, we intend
to discuss language 1) insofar as the general characteristics of expressive life manifest themselves in a very special
way in speech, and 2) insofar as speech occupies a central

---

[1] The author himself did this, as many critics duly noted, in
his work, *Phenomenology of Language*, Duquesne University
Press, 1965.

place in man's expressive life. The proper characteristics of language will be indicated only to the extent that this is necessary for the analysis of the two points to be discussed. Once again, our approach to language, as to expressive life in general, will be inspired by Merleau-Ponty.

In the preceding chapters we drew attention to Merleau-Ponty's strange expression "creation which is, at the same time, adequation," and we mentioned that these words throw light on expressive life in general. They apply also and in particular to language. Language obviously is an "edifice," something built by man, an "edifice" which we construct together. Each one of us enters into a world that has already a language and he gradually learns to situate himself in the common speech. Each one of us also speaks in his own way, and we can often observe that someone gives words a shade of meaning which they did not hitherto possess. Original thinkers and men of letters sometimes introduce even new words, which they need because they have discovered new aspects of reality. The individual's creativity, however, is very restricted with respect to the whole of the language which he speaks.

Language, then, is the result of a common project, a project which we develop together, usually without knowing how we do this. This project, this "creation" is, at the same time an "adequation," for language is, in Heidegger's words, the "home of Being."[2] In language we "bring

[2] "Man is not merely a living being which, in addition to other abilities, also possesses speech. Rather, speech is the home of Being, in which man, while dwelling there, ec-sists by listening to the truth of Being as its shepherd." Heidegger, *Ueber den Humanismus*, Klostermann, Frankfurt a.M., 1947, pp. 21 f. "Even the expression 'home of Being' does not produce a concept of the essence of language—to the dismay of the philosophers,

that which *is* to speech":[3] we let reality speak. Even as in seeing and in the art of painting, which is an extension of seeing, we visualize reality, so also do we verbalize it in speech. For this reason we must be strongly aware of the fact that in our speaking we should be faithful to reality. One can lie, of course, that is, pretend that he gives voice to reality while he deliberately deviates from it. But anyone knows that his speech is then not what it should be.

A fundamental question about language is how it is possible that man expresses reality in a human "edifice," a structure erected by man. This question refers here to language but, as we saw, far exceeds language. In many of our intentional activities we are constructive, but in such a way that our constructions bring reality to light. By seeing, we both constitute a visual field and appropriate the world. The same occurs when we hear, touch, taste, in short, in any of our perceptions. Likewise, in our affective and emotional activities, in which we let reality's attractiveness come to light. And, again, in our admiration and our artistic activities, by which we disclose the world as beautiful.

This phenomenon, our bringing reality to light, is accomplished in a very special way when we speak. In speech the constructive character of our activity is so obvious that, with respect to speech, hardly anyone would be tempted to hold fast to the realistic theory of knowledge as a mirror image of reality. Such a theory, as we mentioned, has sometimes been defended concerning vision: our visual images would be mirror images of a

---

whose discouragement can only see a degeneration of thought in the use of such expressions." Heidegger, *Unterwegs zur Sprache,* Neske, Pfullingen, 1959, p. 112.

[3] "The expression 'to bring to speech' must be understood quite literally. Being comes to speech while it lights up." Heidegger, *Ueber den Humanismus,* p. 45.

ready-made visual field. But, so far as I know, no one has ever considered language as a mere reflection of reality.[4]

In spite of the constructive character of the language we speak, the claim that in this activity we are in touch with *reality* manifests itself here more than anywhere else. People, for instance, who talk about an accident which they have witnessed do not doubt that they are discussing a real event. When one of them makes an incorrect statement, the others will correct him in the name of what objectively happened. To this we must add that the claim of speech to refer to reality extends over an enormous field: in our speaking we refer to all possible kinds of reality, the near-by and the distant, the present and the past, and even the future insofar as it begins to be predelineated in the present. Ordinary speech is refined, methodically perfected and expanded by all kinds of means in the sciences. The sciences devote themselves to everything: there are specialists in practically every old culture of which something remains, in every period of history, every kind of reality, many aspects of human life. Subjectivistically inclined philosophers may doubt whether we can express reality, but the men of science themselves do not have any doubt.[5] Religious people are even convinced

[4] Wittgenstein, however, goes very far when in his *Tractatus logico-philosophicus*, 3.21, he says: "The configuration of 85 objects in a situation corresponds to the configuration of simple signs in the propositional sign." He himself later abandoned this "realism of language," which his commentators generally do not admire.

[5] "Nous voyons les choses mêmes, le monde est cela que nous voyons: des formules de ce genre expriment une foi qui est commune à l'homme naturel et au philosophe dès qu'il ouvre les yeux, elles renvoient à une assise profonde d' 'opinions' muettes impliquées dans notre vie. Mais cette foi a ceci d'étrange que, si l'on cherche à l'articuler en thèse ou énoncé, si l'on se demande ce que c'est que *nous*, ce que c'est que *voir*, et ce que c'est que *chose* ou *monde*, on entre dans un labyrinthe de difficultés et de contradictions." *Le visible et l'invisible*, p. 18.

that they can indicate in their words the religious depth-dimension of life and the world. All this shows that in language we are dealing with a "creation" which is at the same time an "adequation." There is no need to point out that we can be, and often are, mistaken in our speaking, but the very fact that we distinguish between true speech and error indicates that "adequation" is a fundamental characteristic of speech.

It is not necessary to turn to science in order to establish the fact that speech has this fundamental characteristic. For, as we mentioned, scientific speaking is a developent and refinement of ordinary speech. The fundamental characteristics of speech occur also in our ordinary speech: the latter, too, is a human project, a "creation," and this project has the character of an "adequation." These two aspects and their essential connection manifest themselves also in this that speaking is both a making-common and a disclosing or unveiling of being-common. Speech both constitutes and discovers this community.[6]

2. THE STRUCTURE AND INTENTIONALITY OF SPEECH

It is amazing how much man can do with the poor material he has to use when he speaks. In many forms of expression the materials used have a solid material density, but in speech the "material" is "almost nothing." One who pays attention only to the material of language, divorced from its meaning, is left with nothing but a few sounds. We experience this when we hear people speak a language that is totally foreign to us. Precisely, however, because the matter of speech has hardly any material

[6] *Le visible et l'invisible*, pp. 185–187. In a note Merleau-Ponty says that it is a typically Western phenomenon to make a problem of our knowledge of other human beings. See *ibid.*, p. 274.

density, there is much room for man's organizing project. A glance at a dictionary is enough to show what man can do with two dozen elements of sound: they make possible a richly variegated order in which sounds become words, words become sentences, and sentences become a discourse. The structure resulting from those two dozen sounds is so rich that the linguistic sciences, with their many specializations, know that they are still far from having reached the limits.

The richness of this structure, however, does not explain the fact that man can do so much with so little "matter." The explanation should be sought, as Merleau-Ponty indicates, in a different direction. Let us assume that someone points to something with the index finger of his outstretched arm. We would hardly understand anything of this pointing if we merely saw the pointing arm as a thing among things and expressed its pointing movement in an appropriate mathematical formula. True, the body can be considered as an object, and its motions can then be studied just like all other motions. But, by doing so, we would lose sight of the essential element of the arm's motion, viz., that it points. If we wish to understand pointing as pointing, we must not see the pointing body as an object but as a subject. Pointing implies a subject who points, and for this reason only certain motions have the character of pointing. Moreover, pointing is inconceivable unless there is something which is pointed to. And that which is pointed to always belongs to a field of meaning. I cannot point something out to someone unless the two of us exist together in a common field of meaning, no matter how primitive this field may be. The subject who points and that which is pointed to belong to the essence of pointing itself; in other words, pointing simply does not exist without these two.

The same idea applies also to speech. If we limit our

consideration to that of the poverty of the "matter" and the richness of its structure, we lose sight of speech and language in the proper and full sense of the term. It is possible, of course, to center one's attention upon the structure; as a matter of fact, much useful work is done in this way by linguistic sciences. But they keep, at least tacitly, in mind that they are dealing with the structure of something, viz., of language. Any linguist does so as a matter of course, even if he pays no special attention to it, for otherwise he could not speak of the meanings of words. Just as there is no pointing unless someone points and something is pointed to, so also words have no meaning unless there is someone who uses them to signify and something that is signified.

It is true, of course, that what once has been spoken can be repeated. So-called "sedimentation" is an essential possibility of speech. But this phenomenon is only of secondary importance, for whatever is repeated must once have been spoken for the first time. Man has learned to lay down his speaking in writing, so that we can become familiar with what people said long ago. But even then we know that there was someone who originally combined the words. The same applies to other forms of expression that are put on audio or video tape: the taped repetition is inconceivable without the one who expressed himself on it. Expression never leads a completely isolated life, divorced from the man who expressed himself. Rather, we should say that, if someone's expression is still active after his death, then he himself continues to be active. This idea is accepted in common parlance, for we say, e.g., that Plato still exercises great influence today. Such an influence is not limited, of course, to verbal expression, but a rather common phenomenon. Our expressions often are able to exist autonomously: the painter's self-expression on canvas makes it possible for him to continue his influence. Once set into motion, our initiatives often continue their influence in a way which we were unable to foresee. Words spoken in a particular situation continue to live in the hearer's memory and may influence his actions long after they were uttered. A story I tell about someone may influence my listeners only much later, perhaps only after my death, when that person applies for a job with one of my listeners.

Sartre, Merleau-Ponty, Simone de Beauvoir and Francis Jeanson have rightly stressed the ambiguous character of man's responsibility. We exist, and what we do or do not do exercises influence in the intersubjective field, but we do not know what our activities will ultimately bring about. We know that we are active and therefore we are responsible. Our responsibility, however, is not concerned with a field that we can survey with all clarity. In our courts of law the question of the ambiguity found in man's responsibility presents itself daily. Often it is the future which decides whether or not we are guilty. We frequently also ask ourselves what effect an expression we have used will have. When we consider expressions made by an absent person, we implicitly include him in our consideration, even if we know little more about him than that these expressions are his. For this reason we also understand expressions better if we know other expressions of the same person or are familiar with his personality. One who studies a thinker of the past will therefore also try to know something about his life. And if unknown important facts of his life are discovered, his expressions often assume a new meaning.

If language can never be totally disconnected from the speaking man, it likewise cannot be divorced from the matter of which it speaks. The word is a sign and, as such, it is meaningless without that which it signifies. The sign and the signified are dialectically related, for the

105

sign, on the one hand, constitutes the signified and, on the other, is dependent upon it. This dependence is obvious: as referring to what it signifies, the sign depends on the signified. But how can we also say that the sign constitutes the signified? Speech brings to light and makes reality come out of its concealedness. Now, there are many ways in which this can be brought about, and reality itself does not determine in which way it will appear to man and, partly, by means of man. By giving meaning to it, we make reality appear, and the way of reality's appearance depends on the meaning given to it. For this reason the signified never coincides with brute reality, with the "in itself." Reality is not there ready-made, and being-signified is not a superadded relation; otherwise the content of the signified would remain the same, whether or not there is such a superadded relation. If Eastern and Western people differ in "wording" reality, it is not merely a matter of expressing the same signification in different systems of signs. If the language, the approach, is different, then reality appears in a different way, so that a different "signified" arises. That which is "worded," then, never coincides with brute reality.

On the other hand, that which is signified, expressed in words, always is related to reality. One can speak, of course, about purely fictitious objects, as is done in science fiction, but no matter how wild that fiction is, its elements are always derived from the real world in which we live. Similarly, mathematics speaks of objects constituted by man's thinking, but there would be no mathematics if man did not live in a quantified world. That which is signified, expressed in words, then, never totally coincides with a brute reality; it is always co-constituted by man, but at the same time, it is always related to the world appearing to man. Our speaking is never a mere mirroring of reality, but it is also true that we can never, not even in our wildest fancies, wholly free ourselves from reality.

The speaking subject, his language and that which is spoken of are indissolubly connected.[7] This connection is not at all surprising to the phenomenological philosopher, for whom intentionality is a fundamental fact. Now, intentionality implies precisely that the subject *is* an intentional orientation to the other-than-himself, that the subject and that to which the subject is orientated are indissolubly united. Language is one of the links between the human subject and his intentional fields. Man uses many different meanings to bring about his intentional contact with the world. He moves in the world, and for this purpose he uses a motorcycle, a car or a plane; in his working contact with the world he uses many different instruments. Both poles of intentional contact are profoundly influenced by the means used for this contact. The moving man and the field of motion, for example, are very different for a pedestrian and for the driver of a car. Similarly, the working man and the world he reworks have become very different because man has changed his means of work from simple instruments to machines. Thus there is nothing strange in the fact that man uses means to develop his intentional contact with the world. Through abstraction, one can consider these means separately, study their structure and describe their history.

Language also is a means through which man actualizes his intentional contact with the world. Having hardly any material density, this means can be used with the greatest flexibility. Man has great power over it and can do much with it. This is the reason why in language man

[7] Merleau-Ponty develops this connection in his article "On the Phenomenology of Language," *Signs*, Northwestern University Press, 1964, pp. 84 ff.

has such a striking control over his intentional contact with the world: he can freely develop this contact because he has so much freedom in the use of language. It is proper to language to unite man with his intentional correlate in such a way that there is a "distance" between him and his correlate, for the word is a sign, pointing to something else. Thus it makes a connection and, at the same time, effects a "distance." Man appropriates that which is expressed in words, but in such a way that at the same time it also remains at a distance from him. Because of this combination of appropriation and distance, it is not surprising that speech gives man so much freedom.

Because speech, as a means connecting man with the world, can be handled as something very plastic, the way in which the world appears to man as the intentional correlate of his speaking will depend to a large extent on man himself. The center of gravity in the intentional correlation lies here in man. Because this avenue of approach offers great freedom of movement, man, by using this freedom, assumes control over the world. Thanks to speech, man becomes more and more a subject, more free, he sets himself more apart from the world as a free subject, he increases his consciousness. Present-day man is so humanized by his speech that he cannot even imagine what the non-speaking man must have been.

The means of approach to reality which is called "language" is used, developed, refined and made more perfect by man in great freedom. It is hardly necessary to remark that all this is not done by the individual man but by all men together. The individual receives his language as a heritage and, unless he is especially gifted, will not add significantly to it. Yet, the development of language is an established fact. We have developed our speaking into literary, poetical and scientific language or rather into many different kinds of scientific language. In addition, there are humoristic speech and the numerous forms of professional speech. The means of approach to reality called "speech" has become an imposing edifice. In the preceding pages we repeatedly emphasized that this means of approach must be seen precisely as a means of approach, i.e.. language must not be divorced from the human subject who uses it or from the reality which is approached through it. The very development of this means, however, has given it a structure of its own which can become the object of a study.

As a matter of fact, speech is the rich and dynamic object of many empirical sciences. It obeys many laws that are proper to means of approach as such. These laws can be discovered by scientific techniques. For example, one can make use of mathematics because in speech there are quantitative phenomena. One can have recourse to electronic machines to determine how often a particular word occurs in a work. Because feed-back plays an essential role in speaking, speech can become a fertile object of cybernetics. Man has, as we said, much control over language as a means of approach and for this reason, when he approaches reality through language, he will continually correct and adapt himself, in keeping with the knowledge he has about the success of his approach. The use of language does not proceed in a rectilinear way but in an ever self-correcting fashion. While we emphasize that language has the character of a means, an intermediary and, therefore, refuse to isolate it, we do not at all wish to deny that this means has a structure of its own. Without that structure, language could not even function as a means, and the richer this structure becomes, the more language can be a means.

Hitherto we have described language as the means through which man appropriates the world, but we also added that language is something that belongs to the community and is creative of community. Generally speaking, we do not as individuals directly approach the material world through language: we approach the world in dialog with our fellowmen, we address ourselves directly to our fellowmen and through them to the material world. Let us not forget that our fellowman belongs to the world and is the greatest wealth to be found in this world. We not only speak *of* our fellowman, as we speak of other realities, but we also speak *to* him, and he speaks to us: he is not only spoken of but also a fellow-speaker.[8] In many cases speech is a speaking together, a dialog. It is within, and by virtue of, this dialog that language develops the rich structure which was pointed out above.

3. SPEECH AND EXPRESSION

With Merleau-Ponty we have emphasized that, thanks to man's expressive life, reality rises to ever new dimensions. This point reveals itself especially in verbal expression. Verbal expression is not the absolute starting point of man's expressive life. There are preverbal forms of expression and there are also forms of expression which do not precede verbal expression but more or less stand side by side with it.[9] It would not be correct to call dancing, music and painting preverbal, for this term would indicate that those forms of expression should find their perfection through speech. It is true, of course, that certain forms of expression reach a higher level by being put into words. For instance, we use our body to measure

---

[8] "Nul locuteur ne parle qu'en se faisant par avance allocutaire . . . et, du même coup, s'institue aussi *délocutaire*." *Le visible et l'invisible*, p. 202.

[9] "Cependant il y a le monde du silence, le monde perçu, du moins, est un ordre ou il y a significations non langagières; oui, des significations non langagières, mais elles ne sont pas pour autant *positives*." *Le visible et l'invisible*, p. 225.

when we throw a stone or cross a busy highway. But this form of measurement is refined and perfected through mathematical verbalization—to such an extent that it can be used for space travel. Other forms of expression, however, are not perfected in the same way by being verbalized. Man can reach a very high level of expression in them without having recourse to verbalization. Rembrandt's paintings, for example, are superior forms of expression which do not need speech. True, a museum guide can usefully speak about them, but the sole purpose of his speech is to let the visitors see what Rembrandt saw. Once they see, the guide's speaking is no longer needed and, if he continues anyhow, he hampers us in our seeing.

Our verbal expression is based on preverbal forms of expression. Psychology could not speak of seeing if man did not see. If our seeing did not visualize the world, our visualization could not be discussed in any science. Our speaking about space presupposes that we give meaning to space by moving in it, by existing in it. Our verbalization of space is based on the fact that we dwell in space—a fact that is sometimes lost sight of in the discussions about space. By verbalizing, we give a new mode of being to a meaning which existed already for us. Speech does not simply make this meaning be, but merely makes it be in a new way.

Our language is full of words which point to preverbal forms of expression. Many words which refer to our thinking, affections and emotions, our so-called "interior life," originally pointed to attitudes and activities of the body. We under*stand*, our decision *stands*, he is an *independent* thinker, I am *stuck* with a problem, *filled* with pity, etc. We exist before we begin to verbalize and the way we exist profoundly influences our mode of verbalization. Usually we are hardly, or not at all, aware of this, for our speaking can easily lead such an autonomous life that we forget its dependence. Speech does not even have to be aware of its dependence in order to function properly. The philosopher, however, who wishes to understand and situate our speaking must pay attention to this dependence.

Expressive life, then, precedes and exceeds verbalization. Even when we speak, our expressive life exceeds the verbalization of our speech. There are, for example, people whose speech usually manifests modesty or arrogance. Others speak in such a way that, even when they have to say something disagreeable, they are listened to with sympathy. Others again make us tend to resist, even if they bring welcome news. Yet, such people do not verbalize their modesty, their arrogance or sympathy. In other words, their speech expresses more than they say. How we express our modesty, arrogance, sympathy or love in such a case is something which usually escapes us. The tone of our voice, the way we participate in the conversation, the way we look while we speak and many other factors play a role in this matter. It is possible to learn how to control one's expressivity in this respect. A good actor, for example, can play the role of either a modest or an arrogant person. A sales representative also can be taught to speak in such a way that people are inclined to listen to him. Similarly, one who holds dictatorial powers can learn to speak so authoritatively that for many people it becomes difficult to contradict him. Nevertheless, we do not succeed in completely controlling our expressive life: even if someone tries to hide his true character, it will reveal itself sooner or later to people who know him well.

In summary, our speaking is expressive not only as the verbalization of what we wish to discuss but also as a form of behavior. While being expressive in its own special way, it also remains expressive in the way gestures and other kinds of behavior are expressive. Thus we must make a distinction between its specific expressivity and the general expressivity which it shares with other forms of behavior. These two forms of expressivity constitute, or at least can constitute, a unit. In a good actor, for example, the expressivity of speech as behavior will underscore the content of his speaking. The same is true for a good teacher: he not only presents his topic in a clear and consistent fashion but also in an agreeable way, so that his students will be inclined to accept it.

All this is rather obvious. When we speak with others we often wish to accomplish something in them that goes beyond a mere rational conviction; for instance, we wish to persuade them to declare themselves in favor of an action to be undertaken or to render a particular service. In such a case it is important that our expressivity be as perfect as possible, and this cannot be attained by paying attention only to the rational consistency of our arguments. Both the general and the special form of expressivity are needed for this purpose, and they must be in harmony. At the same time, it remains true that the special expressivity proper to speech retains the crucial role. If, for example, someone is a master of the expressivity of speech as behavior but has nothing to say, he is not likely to make any lasting impression, no matter how charmingly he may speak. A certain intelligence, however, is needed even to master the expressivity of speech in the general sense: one who is really stupid will show this not only in the content of his speech but also in his behavior.

With respect to education it may be useful to point out that intellectual training which places a one-sided emphasis on verbalization disregards the expressivity of speech as behavior. While this may be relatively harmless for people who will spend their lives in research in a laboratory or a scholar's study, it would be disastrous for one whose function it is to pass on his knowledge to students.

A successful teacher needs more than a good understanding of the subject matter which he teaches.

4. The Proper Character of Verbal Expression

Speaking, we saw, is a form of behavior and as such reveals something about the temperament and the personality of the speaker. The proper character of this behavior, however, is that something is put into words, and this putting-into-words is expression in a very special sense. It is very difficult to indicate exactly what this proper character is. One could suggest that verbal expression be compared with nonverbal expression, so that the difference between them can be described. But such a comparison is not possible because man expresses everything in words and because his speaking permeates his entire existence. The way we see, feel, taste, work, move in traffic, dance or paint is profoundly influenced by verbal expression. Once a form of expression which in itself is nonverbal becomes the object of discussion, we no longer use it in the same way. For example, the way sexual life is spoken of in a group of people profoundly influences the way sex is lived by them. Through speech we correct and perfect many nonverbal forms of expression. "Nonverbal" can be understood in two senses, viz., as referring to a form of expression that in itself is nonverbal, and as referring to one that is not influenced by verbal expression. It is easy to find examples of the former, but among modern adults there are none, or hardly any, of the latter.[10] Examples occur among animals and little children, but they are unable to give us any explanations, and for adults it is exceedingly difficult to "capture" these nonverbal forms of expression from within—precisely because they are nonverbal. In other words, we do not know what a nonverbal field of

[10] *Le visible et l'invisible*, p. 203.

existence is and therefore experience the greatest difficulty in circumscribing the proper character of verbal expression.

Moreover, verbal expression itself assumes an enormous variety of forms. The philosopher who reflects upon verbal expression will be inclined to pay special attention to the form which aims at expressing truth on the scientific or prescientific levels. Speech, however, can primarily aim at expressing moods, it can be a playing with words in which humor predominates, it can manifest one's feelings with respect to other human beings, or reveal one's wishes, desires or orders. This partial enumeration shows the dangers run by one who wishes to describe the proper character of speech: he may consider what is proper to a particular form of verbal expression as the essence of all verbal expression. If, e.g., one says that through verbal expression man elevates himself to the order of truth, one begins by leaving many forms of verbal expression out of consideration. Accordingly, if we wish to speak about the proper character of speech, we are forced to use vague formulas. With due allowance for this vagueness, we may now try to say something about the proper character of verbal expression.

Through verbal expression the meaning that is expressed in it becomes common, for language is by its very nature something common, even though each of the individuals speaks it in his own way. If language were not common, it could not function as a means of communication. That which in any way is verbally expressed begins to lead a common existence, which in principle is open to all. If, e.g., someone sees me doing something blameworthy, I fear less the fact that he saw me—which is a single act—than the speaking which can follow from his seeing. Once he expresses in words what he saw, my action begins to lead a public existence. I cannot ask that witness not to have seen what I did, but I can ask him not to speak.

Secondly, verbal expression raises the level of objectification. It would be wrong to claim that objectification arises only on the level of language, for any intentional activity implies the constituting of a subject and therefore also of an object. In this sense we may even speak of the object of an animal's seeing and desiring. But in speech the word mediates between subject and object. The term "between" could be confusing, for one could think that it refers to a third party between those two. But there is no question of a third in the strict sense of the term: the word is the subject's instrument of approach and as such it lies on the side of the subject. On the other hand, this instrument of the subject has a structure of its own, to such an extent that the subject can reflect upon it, examine it critically and deliberately correct it, as he does today in a scientific fashion. In this way there arises a greater distance between subject and object. The speaking subject distances himself more from what he expresses than does the seeing subject from his field of vision. This comparison, however, could be misunderstood. It can happen that a seer may seem to distance himself just as much from his field of vision; for example, when he "deciphers" this field with almost scientific precision, as a pilot does who looks at his instrument panel when a red light begins to burn there. But when the seer distances himself so much from his field of vision, language has already performed its intermediary function: the pilot looks for something to which we have already given a name.

Because it is possible for us to manipulate language, we can also exercise a profound influence on the way reality will appear to us. For example, by using scientific language, we constitute reality as a field of scientific thought. The reality appearing to us does not coincide with the field of thought of, e.g., the physical sciences, but we constitute reality as a field of this kind of scientific thinking. We are able to limit ourselves in what we wish to consider and divide it from what we wish to leave aside. Speech is a powerful means of self-limitation which leads to greater control. There is also a limit when we see, taste or feel reality, but it is a limitation over which we have no control; hence we may not use the term "self-limitation" here. But the possibility of self-limitation given in speech, or rather, which we give ourselves by creating our language, gives rise to the sciences. Let us add that this self-limitation is not merely found in the sciences: the humorist and the satirist also limit themselves by means of speech.

Thirdly, speech not only raises the level of objectification but also that of subjectification, for these two are indissolubly connected. One who is already a subject becomes more a subject by learning to speak. In former times the soul, spirit or subject was too much viewed as an ontological given which is or is not. Today we have a more dynamic view, which makes it possible to speak of the subject's coming to be. Merleau-Ponty views the duality of subject and object as a dualization. (He himself does not use this term, but it aptly expresses his intention.) As we pointed out, a dualization occurs when a part of visible reality becomes seeing. This dualization, however, can also reach a higher level, and it does so by virtue of our speaking. The subject then becomes more subject, and the object more object. If one wishes to use the term "interiorization" to indicate this constituting of the subject —for the subject is "with" the other-than-self in such a way that he is also with himself—he can say that through speech interiorization reaches a higher level.

All this is rather obvious. We begin by speaking with others: the child learns to speak in intersubjective contact.

117

But when through contact with others we have learned to speak, we can also speak in ourselves, without addressing ourselves to others: the subject's dialog with others then makes way for the inner dialog of the subject with himself. This inner dialog occupies an important place in human existence. At a certain stage of his development the young human being reaches this interiorization. We do not mean that without speech there is no interiorization, but only that interiorization reaches a higher level through speech. Instead of speaking of a development of interiorization, one could also use the term "developing" or "growing consciousness."

Finally, man owes a new form of freedom to language, for he becomes more free according as he can distance himself more from his situation. This ability to distance himself is a condition that is presupposed by control over the situation. Because language places man at a distance from his situation in a new way, it also gives him more freedom. This freedom reveals itself also in the fact that, thanks to language, we are not limited to "here and now." Man is able to evoke the absent, the near and distant past, and make them appear to his presence. Although memory precedes language, it is to a large extent actualized through speech. One notices this when he has forgotten certain words by which realities are indicated: he then has the feeling that these realities themselves escaped him. This is a clear indication that language is a powerful means at the service of memory: it serves to fix and lay hold of the past. This is why we establish files in which we put down on paper whatever happens in industry and society at large. By verbalizing the past on paper, we are able to hold on to it. Without the aid of language we would not be able to fix the flowing stream of events as we actually do.

This description of the specific character of language

leaves us with the uncomfortable feeling that it remains on the periphery of a core which we would like to grasp, but which our words fail to capture. By speaking we express—but what? Certainly not a finished interiority which we find in ourselves. We express that of which we speak, and the topic of our speech is usually something existing outside our speaking. It is something "given," i.e., we generally realize that it was "there" before we began to speak of it. Yet, language is precisely expression because we make the given exist in a new way for us. If the verbal expression is successful, we usually realize that we have captured in words something that was already "there" but, at the same time, we also realize that we never saw this given reality as we see it now thanks to our verbalization. While speaking we ex-plain, unfold, that is, we indicate one feature after the other; we do so not only in scientific speech but also in other forms of speaking, such as a simple story of what happened or a humorous description.

We speak about a topic by expressing ourselves in many words. Because there are many words, our speaking is an analysis, and because these words are connected we make a synthesis. Speech is always both analysis and synthesis, or at least an attempt to analyze and synthetize. Speech is expression precisely because the topic is captured in a plurality of connected words, albeit that the attempt can be more or less successful or even wholly unsuccessful. The complex of linguistic signs does not become a substitute for the reality we wish to express, for this complex refers to that reality and would become meaningless without that reference. One who listens to a complex of linguistic signs and does not succeed in recognizing in it a reference to a reality does not have the feeling that he is listening to genuine speech. Speech is essentially intentional, it has to be concerned with something, and what it is concerned with must disclose itself in speech.

One may wonder why in these few remarks about speech as expression nothing has been said about the concept. With Merleau-Ponty, we reject the view that, wholly divorced from language, there is in us a concept mirroring the thing understood and that speech is the expression of such an internal mirroring. Obviously, we do not intend to deny concepts, but we refuse to see in the concept an internal reality distinct from the thing understood and distinct also from verbal expression. Rather, the concept is the interiority of our very speaking. Speaking is not merely "body," but also has a "soul." The concept is this soul, this "other side of the body," without which the "body" of language would not be itself. While speaking, we understand, or rather, we begin to understand, and without understanding—concepts—there is not even any speaking. The concept belongs to the very essence of speech.[11]

5. LANGUAGE AND IDEA

This most intimate bond between speech and concept becomes perhaps somewhat more intelligible if we pay attention to Merleau-Ponty's remarks about the nonabstract ideas encountered in music, literature and the life of love.[12] He gives credit in this matter to Proust, who drew attention to this viewpoint before him. It is not easy,

---

[11] "Die Kraft des Geistes ist nur so gross als ihere Aeusserung, seine Tiefe nur so tief, als er in seiner Auslegung sich auszubreiten und sich zu verlieren getraut." Hegel, *Phaenomenologie des Geistes*, ed. by Hoffmeister, p. 15.

[12] "La littérature, la musique, les passions, mais aussi l'expérience du monde visible, sont non moins que la science de Lavoisier et d'Ampère l'exploration d'un invisible et, aussi bien qu'elle, dévoilement d'un univers d'idées." *Le visible et l'invisible*, p. 196.

however, to express in a rational way what Proust and Merleau-Ponty mean. It can easily happen that a melody seizes us and for a considerable time keeps us in its power. Even a simple melody can do this. What is such a melody? A succession of a few sounds, but it resounds deeply in us, it puts us in a special mood, it colors our world, it influences the way we exist, it calms us when we are excited, it fascinates us. Such a melody undoubtedly has depth and finds resonance in the mysterious depth of our life. We cannot give a rational expression either to the depth dimension of the melody or to that of our own existence in which the melody speaks to us.

The same phenomenon manifests itself in the sphere of love and friendship. A particular encounter with a fellow-man can move us very deeply. Few words perhaps were spoken, and a gesture may have been more important than all the words we exchanged. Somehow, a contact which, on the surface, seemed shallow had depth and spoke to us on a level so deep that it defies rational reflection. This can even happen with respect to characters in a novel: the two main figures in Dostoevski's *Crime and Punishment*, Raskolnikov and Sonja, can touch a reader to the core of his being. The same phenomenon can also occur with respect to people in the public eye, e.g., John F. Kennedy and Pope John XXIII. There are many people who are in the public eye, of course, but these two found an echo in the hearts of many. Why? We do not succeed if we try to find a rational explanation. Yet, there was a contact-in-depth with them and no one doubts this, even if we cannot find a rational explanation. A similar depth is also found in the sexual relationship of people who authentically love each other, in the birth of a child, and in many other events and encounters.

The depth dimension of such appearing reality has an ideal character. Something appears to us in the perceptible order, for we enter into contact with that reality by seeing, listening or reading. The perceptible surface, however, is not at all identical with the appearing reality. There is a contact that touches us to the core, and we know that this is not merely a subjective impression but that we are being influenced by the invisible depth-dimension of appearing reality itself. There is here, says Merleau-Ponty, an "invisible" aspect which is the "other side" of the "visible." The visible would not be what it is without this invisible other side.[13] It is wholly impossible, however, to separate the two dimensions from each other. The idea essentially leads a material existence:[14] it is incorporated and cannot be divorced from its embodiment. Without sounds there is no melody. Love and friendship reveal themselves essentially in the way one encounters his fellowman; they become only real within the actual encounter. There are people who would like to be lovers of each other or friends but do not succeed. In such a case there is no question of a love or friendship that is innerly already there but unable to find expression, but rather of a capacity that remains unrealized. If one tries to express the power of attraction of John F. Kennedy or Pope John in an abstract formula, this power is lost in the formula, except for those who retain a lively memory of these persons; the abstract formula then owes its light to this con-

---

[13] "Comme la noirceur secrète du lait, dont Valéry a parlé, n'est accessible qu'à travers sa blancheur, l'idée de la lumière ou l'idée musicale doublent par en dessous les lumières et les sons, en sont l'autre coté ou la profondeur." *Le visible et l'invisible*, pp. 197 f.

[14] "L'idée est ce niveau, cette dimension, non pas donc un invisible de fait, comme un objet caché derrière un autre, et non pas un invisible absolu, qui n'aurait rien à faire avec le visible, mais l'invisible *de* ce monde, celui qui l'habite, le soutient et le rend visible, sa possibilité intérieure et propre, l'Être de cet étant." *Ibid.*, p. 198.

crete remembrance, and not vice versa. In all these cases we are dealing with something belonging to the realm of the spirit which is essentially connected with its embodiment and appears by virtue of this embodiment. The spirit is here really the "other side" of the body, the idea discloses itself in matter, and any abstract explicitation, says Merleau-Ponty, does not offer us the idea itself but only a second version of it, a derivative expression which can be handled more easily.[15] The ideas themselves are offered to us only in a "fleshly experience."[16] All this belongs to the essence of any kind of art. In the world of art we meet the sublime far more than in the sphere of abstractions, for the sublime offers itself only in "bodily contact."

Such ideas, says Merleau-Ponty, have far more power than abstract ideas. With respect to the latter, we can say that *we* possess them, but the former possess *us*. An abstract idea does not keep us fascinated: once we have it, we quickly pass on to search for other ideas.[17] Nonabstract ideas can occupy us for a long time and, as it were, obsess us.[18] People who are captivated by a particular melody will over and over again replay its recording and call it their favored melody. They are not interested in an abstract description of what they experience.

These ideas, says Merleau-Ponty, offer us the consolation that the flesh is not without spirit or soul, that appearing reality has a spiritual depth, and that in the density of

[15] "L'explicitation ne nous donne pas l'idée même, elle n'en est qu'une version seconde, un dérivé plus maniable." *Le visible et l'invisible*, p. 197.

[16] *Ibid.*, p. 197.

[17] "Une pensée positive est ce qu'elle est, mais, précisément, n'est que cela, et dans cette mesure elle ne peut nous fixer. Déjà la volubilité de l'esprit le mène ailleurs." *Ibid.*, p. 198.

[18] "Les idées musicales ou sensibles, précisément parce qu'elles sont négativité ou absence circonscrite, nous ne les possédons pas, elles nous possèdent." *Ibid.*, pp. 198 f.

our own flesh there is a depth that can resound with the depth of appearing reality.[19]

Once a person has experienced this kind of "ideality," says Merleau-Ponty, he will not easily be inclined to give it up;[20] on the contrary, he will endeavor to explain all "ideality" in this fashion. Thus we must ask whether such an explanation is possible. There are abstract ideas which, it seems, will resist that kind of an explanation. For abstract ideas rise above "here and now"; moreover, philosophers used to speak about total abstraction from all materiality. Are not the bonds existing between abstract ideas purely intelligible bonds, absolutely necessary bonds which are independent of matter? Does not formal logic pursue precisely this kind of purely intelligible connections which transcend the entire order of what actually is?

Yet, it is possible to reply that our abstract ideas also are not without "world," without "flesh."[21] For they are embodied in a language, even if that language consist of mathematical signs. True, the "body" in question is then rather subtle and constituted by ourselves; nevertheless, it is a "body." This body does not come to be and pass away with this or that individual perceptive experience. Once the signs are constituted, they can be used again and again, they can be fixed in our memory or on paper. The "body" in question continues to exist, even when the one who planned it has disappeared, for it is an inter-subjective body which, in principle, is accessible to everyone.

Thus, may we not see abstract "ideality" as the "other

---

[19] "Elles nous donnent l'assurance que la 'grande nuit impénétrée et décourageante de notre âme' n'est pas vide, n'est pas néant." *Ibid.*, p. 197.

[20] *Ibid.*, p. 199.

[21] "Disons seulement que l'idéalité pure n'est pas elle-même sans chair ni délivrée des structures d'horizon: elle en vit, quoiqu'il s'agisse d'une autre chair et d'autres horizons." *Ibid.*, p. 200.

side" of this body? Is not the idea or concept the interiority of speaking itself? Such assertions remain unintelligible for one who starts from the *a priori* assumption that the interiority of thought is distinct from the exteriority of the word. Once interiority is placed outside the word, the latter can, of course, be nothing but a poor reference which does not have any density in itself. If the word is conceived in this way, it becomes utterly impossible to ascribe any interiority to speech itself. The result is an impoverished view of what language is, but that hypothesis on which the view is based is simply posited *a priori*.

The objection could be raised that Merleau-Ponty's concept of language is just as much posited *a priori*. The reply is that Merleau-Ponty at least based himself on analogies which point in the direction of his view. The meaning of gestures, dance, melody, painting and sculpture cannot be separated from the "flesh" in which they are given. They are, in his terms, ideality interwoven with the flesh. If, then, we encounter both ideality and flesh in the realm of abstract ideas, why should we suddenly separate these two in this realm? There appears to be no reason for such a sudden difference.

One could say that abstract ideality represents a higher order and that, therefore, it is not surprising to find here characteristics which do not appear in the lower regions of ideality. This objection, however, fails to convince because it does not justify its claim that embodied ideality is simply a lower form of ideality. Why should the ideality of music be *per se* of a lower level than that of abstract thought? Why should the visualization of reality embodied in a painting by Rembrandt be *per se* of a lower level than that of a book written by a scientific genius? In the ideality which is indissolubly united with the "flesh" we often encounter, as we said, the sublime. There is no reason to qualify this sublime element as lower than abstract thought. The very terms "higher" and "lower" can be dangerous, they can express an *a priori* established hierarchy that is imposed on reality in an unjustified way.

It would be better simply to say that these spheres of ideality are different, without attempting to arrange them in a hierarchical order. This assertion does not imply nominalism in the bad sense of the term.[22] One who speaks of nominalism in the bad sense has already separated concept and word, and on this basis he despises those who admit nothing but words. Such nominalists, then, are taken to really deny the concept. We, however, do not at all deny the concept, but only its proclaimed divorce from the word.

In our discussion of language we almost involuntarily began to describe language as it is used in scholarly philosophy, in spite of the fact that we had warned against the danger of such a restriction. Yet, how can one who reflects upon language avoid placing in the foreground his own way of using language? One could also place the poetic or the humoristic use of language in the foreground. No one doubts that, just as there are ingenious men of learning, so also there are ingenious poets and ingenious humorists. They, too, are users of language, and it would be wrong to say that their use is on a lower level than that of a man of science. Now, who would ever separate the meaning of the poet's or the humorist's speaking from their speaking itself? It makes no sense to put the meaning of poetic or humoristic speech as an abstract concept outside their speaking itself. If one deprives the poet or the humorist of his language, nothing remains of them. Word and meaning here just as evidently compenetrate each other as the meaning of dancing and body movements, as the meaning of a painting and the painted canvas. Why, then, should

[22] "Le nominalisme a raison: les significations ne sont que des *écarts définis.*" *Ibid.*, p. 291.

we accept that in abstract thinking alone there exist a separation between word and concept which does not occur anywhere else? With Merleau-Ponty, therefore, we may conclude that the concept is the interiority of speech. But let us emphasize once again that, without this interiority, speech is an empty playing with sound.

6. THE PRIVILEGED POSITION OF VERBAL EXPRESSION

In the preceding pages we spoke of the position of verbal expression within the totality of man's expressive life, and it became gradually clear that verbal expression is only one among the many ways in which man expresses himself. Verbal expression, nevertheless, occupies a very special position in the totality of our expressive life: while being one among many ways of self-expression, all the others can somehow be transposed into language. This assertion should be evident from the situation of expressive life in today's society. There is hardly a form of expression for which there is no institute or school where one can devote himself to it: there are schools of drama, institutes for plastic arts, academies of sculpture, dance institutes, etc. In addition to practical exercise, these schools also give theoretical instruction. In other words, they verbalize these nonverbal forms of expression.

Practically everything is verbalized by man. There exists no important phenomenon that is not the object of scientific inquiry, and any important form of human *praxis* is discussed by a corresponding science. Not every verbalization, however, is equally successful. It stands to reason that it succeeds better in mathematics than with respect to dancing, music or painting. The latter, in final analysis, defy verbalization with respect to their most specific character: one has to see, hear or experience them.

Verbalization, nevertheless, remains an important means, first, for learning to see or hear, secondly, for criticizing and correcting one's expression and thus raising it to a higher level. We use verbalization almost everywhere and find it useful. Thus we cannot disregard the question how this is possible.

Man's reason obviously is at work not only in verbal expression but in all expressive forms that are genuinely human. As we mentioned before, little children and animals play, but at a given moment man begins to organize his playing in the light of reason. Reason is at work in music and dance, in painting, sculpturing, art photography, etc. One can apply here the old saying that reason is the principle of order. It is only in verbal expression, however, that reason can become pure and rigorous reason. In the other forms of expression it operates as "enlarged reason." On the basis of pure reason man cannot dance, compose music, sculpture a statue or paint. These forms of expression need more than pure reason, and this "more" can be called "artistic sensitivity," "artistic ability," etc. We could say that in the nonverbal forms of expression—and also in the artistic verbal expression—reason operates in a more latent way, which less clearly reveals itself as reason.

It should be evident that the explicitation of the element of reason can render good service in the development of the nonverbal expression. For through this explicitation the organizing function of reason is brought into focus. Now, it is through verbal expression that the element of reason is explicitated. In verbal expression we distance ourselves from the actual expression in order to express how the latter operates. We explicitly focus our attention upon the rational order which remains more or less hidden in the actual expression. It goes without saying that, by doing this, we foster the activity of organizing reason.

The rational verbal expression, therefore, can render service to the other forms of expression. By means of such a reflection we can, e.g., indicate the fundamental melody of a musical composition and show how the composition is built around that fundamental melody. Or, one can point out the function of measure and rhythm. All this serves to make people aware of the order established by reason and this can also to a certain extent help to improve this order.

It must be pointed out, however, that rational reflection alone is of little help, for with respect to nonverbal expression the strictly rational is never the essential. Only one who has a feeling for the essential dimension of such a form of expression can be aided by rational reflection. For example, one who is bereft of any feeling for music can still learn everything which rational reflection knows about music. He could perhaps even discuss these rational reflections, but he would be like one born blind who discusses vision: the proper element remains a closed book to him, and rational reflections do not enable him to accomplish anything in the realm of musical self-expression. Thus one can understand why artists are suspicious of rational reflection: the latter is dangerous when one does not realize how relative its value is with respect to artistic expression. The rational discussion of art should be borne by esthetic sensitivity; it is this sensitivity, and not rational reflection which is the norm of art. The sciences that devote themselves to art can render great service to it, provided they remain modest. New ways in art do not, as a rule, arise from rational reflection, but are born in living art itself. In spite of the temptation to explore this matter further because of its rich possibilities, we shall not do it here. All we wished to do here was to clarify that rational verbalization can render important services to other forms of expression.

There remains one final question about verbal expression. Merleau-Ponty, we saw, uses the peculiar sentence: "Being perceives in us," the visible becomes in us a seeing of itself. This statement is not peripheral with respect to Merleau-Ponty's view, one could even say that his reflection culminates in it. He applies this statement also to verbal expression and says: "Being speaks in us." What sense, if any, does such a statement have? Let us begin by observing that one who really tries to give expression to reality is not, or rather should not be, concentrated on himself. Sometimes one meets speakers who are visibly much pleased with themselves. They discuss a topic, but it is evident that what interests them most is not the topic but the pleasure they experience in being able to speak so well about it. Obviously, what is expected of a speaker is that he discusses a topic for its own sake and not for his personal honor and glory. He has, of course, the right to be recognized if he puts forward new ideas, but the actual expression of his ideas should not be centered on this right. In authentic self-expression the speaker's attention is focussed on the topic he wishes to discuss.

As a matter of fact, great creative minds often deny themselves much in their personal existence in order to give expression to reality. They act as if they place themselves fully at the disposal of what they express. It even happens rather frequently that physicians try in vain to moderate intellectuals who devote themselves wholly to study or research. The same phenomenon occurs also among others who pursue different forms of expression. Much personal happiness has been sacrificed on the altar of art. A very one-sided life is often the fate of people who reach greatness in any particular form of expression: they neglect other values which normally occupy a place in the life of cultured man. One could claim that such people invert the hierarchy of values: science, art, etc. are for the sake of man, but they seem to live for the sake of science or art. But, is such a claim correct? The value such people pursue is something that transcends individual existence: the light sought by the man of science is not just his light but light for all. He takes part in mankind's common task to bring reality to light. It is not inhuman for man to place his life at the service of suprapersonal values.[23]

We may add that this suprapersonal character belongs essentially to most forms of work. The engineers who plan and build a giant dam do not labor solely for something that concerns their own individual existence. Even in the simple planting of fruit trees it is proverbial that the father plants trees of which his children will gather the fruit. The world of work becomes wholly unintelligible if one demands that the individual devote himself only to values and products that serve his own individual existence. The individual, we think, can become great only by devoting himself to suprapersonal values, and his life shrinks to insignificance if he does not do this. Expression becomes unintelligible if the individual expressing himself is solely concerned with himself.

Man *is* existence which brings light: in him and through him reality becomes a light. This statement is very much applicable also to verbal expression, and it was this Merleau-Ponty had in mind when he said that "Being speaks in us." To be a light-bringing existence is for man not only a given but also a task. Wherever he sees any possibility of bringing reality to light in a new way, he will make use of it. His motivation in this is not purely practical or economic. True, economic considerations exercise great influence, but they cannot explain everything. There are many investigations that do not offer any economic promises, yet they are pursued in our universities. No faculty would tolerate a condition in which academic

[23] "Ce n'est pas moi qui me fais penser, pas plus que ce n'est moi qui fais battre mon coeur." *Le visible et l'invisible*, p. 275.

pursuits are solely dominated by economic considerations: they would condemn such a condition as a violation of the value of knowledge.

It would be useless to try to convince people that by now man knows enough about any topic. "Enough" is a term that does not fit knowledge. The question of what one can do with a particular type of knowledge may impress people who are wholly "practical" and therefore inclined to laugh at academic pursuits, but it fails to impress genuine men of scholarship: to bring reality to light is a vocation to which man is called by the very fact of being-man. Obviously, not all men work at this vocation in the above-mentioned way. Together we must realize many values: bringing reality to light is only one of these, albeit not the least of them. It is useless also to point out that art, science and philosophy will overtake the work of the individual, that sooner or later his work will be antiquated. Everyone knows this, but it does not make him stop his work, for his work is not concerned with himself as an individual only. We are at the service of a value which transcends us as individuals and we know that we, as individual persons, can have a meaningful existence precisely because of our dedication to that value. Man is too great to be contained in egocentrism.

Why is man called to bring reality to light? Simply because he is man, because he is a light-bringing existence. He is the one through whom and in whom reality becomes visible to itself. Man finds satisfaction in this light that transcends him.

It stands to reason that much more can be said about verbal expression. We had to limit ourselves here, however, because we spoke about verbal expression within the broader framework of man as expression.

CHAPTER SIX

Actual Problems of Expressive Life

1. THE PREDOMINANCE OF SCIENCE

WITHIN THE limited framework of this book it is not possible to discuss all forms of expressive life in detail. We have devoted a special chapter to verbal expression because the latter occupies such a central position, and in the final chapter we will speak more specifically about religious expression, which today arouses considerable interest. In this chapter, however, we will reflect upon the actual problems encountered in expressive life.

That there really are problems is a matter of record. All kinds of institutes have arisen which devote themselves to problems of expression, particularly in connection with education. Examining their own school days, today's adults judge that their education was one-sided with respect to the development of their expressive abilities and they wish to avoid the same mistake in the education of their children. What are the reasons why they plead in favor of more space for playfulness and for artistic formation in modern education? Why do they found special institutes for expression?

The one-sidedness against which the protest is raised can easily be observed. Verbal expression, in particular its scientific form, largely dominates expressive life. The reason is that science has become an economic factor of the first order. Science has existed for at least two thousand years, but only in the past fifty years has education in science become a more general phenomenon. In former times science played no role in material production. True, man is able to produce things because he is endowed with reason, he approaches the world with reason. At first, however, he worked by the light of prescientific reason, while today his work is guided by scientific reason. Everything indicates that in the future scientific reason will increasingly guide man in his productive work. The new science of cybernetics draws much attention: it studies and produces self-regulating processes by means of so-called "feed-back." The intention is to make production a self-regulating process, so that man can leave to machines not only the work of his hands but also certain tasks of his intellect. All this, of course, is possible only because of science, and science here means primarily the exact sciences. For this reason modern society is willing to make enormous investments of money in scientific research and scientific training.[1] It is an investment in the economic value of science, for those who make the investment are convinced that they will get very substantial returns on the capital spent.

Scientific education, then, occupies a larger place than ever before, and its place is destined to become even greater. One can see this in the development of educational institutions. A school is no longer called good unless the exact sciences are taught well in superbly equipped laboratories. Junior colleges arise everywhere to satisfy the demand for skilled personnel, and university graduates with an M.Sc. or a Ph.D. in the exact sciences can afford to be very choosy about their jobs. Books and

[1] Western Europe still lags far behind the United States and the U.S.S.R. in this matter.

articles publishing research in the exact sciences have become so numerous that even experts in the field sometimes are unable to know whether or not a particular problem has already been investigated.

There are many people who protest against the one-sided predominance of the exact sciences. This protest is not directed against these sciences as such and their development, for everyone realizes that life literally depends on them today. The protest is against the fact that other aspects of life do not receive their due because of the one-sided emphasis on science.

This protest is one of the central themes of Merleau-Ponty's philosophy. He does not deny the value of science —although he should perhaps have taken care to make this point more explicit. But he refuses to identify the light of speech with scientific speaking. Science, he says, is operationalistic: it works with models and wishes to make these models effective. The question of truth is something in which it is less and less interested. Thus the danger is not at all imaginary that nature will be reduced to object X of man's operations.[2] Science, moreover, is a strongly channelized approach to reality: it thinks in quantitative categories and, if it looks at qualitative aspects of reality, it considers them in the light of those quantitative categories. Besides, science does not have its foundation in itself, for the scientific discussion of reality is always a development of man's prescientific speaking of reality. Although scientific speaking enormously develops and refines certain aspects of prescientific speaking, it neglects other aspects.

[2] "Dire que le monde *est* par définition nominale l'objet X de nos opérations, c'est porter à l'absolu la situation de connaissance du savant, comme si tout ce qui fut ou est n'avait jamais été que pour entrer au laboratoire." Merleau-Ponty, *L'oeil et l'esprit*, p. 11.

Thus we may never call the scientific approach to reality *the* approach without any qualification. Philosophy must busy itself also with science, but it may not make science its foundation and starting point, for otherwise it would base itself on too narrow an approach. Insofar as science has the tendency to equate knowledge with scientific knowledge, the philosopher has the duty to reject and oppose this claim. Merleau-Ponty wanted to let his philosophical look penetrate particularly into the dark soil in which science is rooted—and not science alone but also art, work and the entire expressive life of man. He wanted to recover man's most primordial contact with the world, a contact which, on the one hand, is semidarkness and, on the other, is not yet touched by the one-sidedness of man's more refined and developed approaches. This chapter, then, is written in the spirit of Merleau-Ponty, although we will pay attention to other aspects than those he considered.

Not only a philosophy like that of Merleau-Ponty but also many publications about expression, in particular those which pursue a practical aim, argue against the one-sided emphasis on science. This is not surprising, for the plea to make more room for the cultivation of expression, e.g., in high school, has per force to attack the tendency of the sciences to demand all available time for themselves. It is true, of course, that the sciences themselves also are a form of expression. This is a point that is sometimes overlooked by those who wish to make more room for the cultivation of expression. One may even say that science is an extremely important form of expression. For this reason it is wrong to oppose the cultivation of expression to the pursuit of the sciences. One who wishes to reserve the term "expression" for nonscientific endeavors shows that he does not appreciate science as he should.

Scientific expressivity experiences a period of bloom in

our days. It arises from a critical purification of the use we make of language, a task in which all great men of science take part. This purification and refinement, through which speaking becomes scientific speaking, is not limited to the actual pursuit of science, but is also the topic of reflection in logic, a discipline that dates back thousands of years. Even in antiquity abstraction was made from content and the question was then raised what demands had to be satisfied in order that speech could be called "scientific." For centuries, Aristotle was considered the grand master of logic, but in our era logic experiences a new period of bloom and explores the laws of thinking far beyond the dreams of the ancients. There exists, moreover, a valuable branch of philosophical reflection which helps us to purify also our philosophical speech, viz., analytic philosophy. It arose from the discovery that philosophical problems often also suffer from impure ways of speaking and therefore analytic philosophy made a study of the language used in philosophy. It soon appeared that logicians and analytic philosophers could collaborate fruitfully. In short, much effort is being devoted to the purification and refinement of scientific speaking, and this effort contributes very much to scientific speech. Scientific expression, then, should be recognized as a genuine form of expression.

2. RETURN TO THE BODY

What exactly is wanted by those who protest against the one-sided predominance of science and its technology? Merleau-Ponty's philosophical orientation offers an indication: it is largely concerned with the consciousness of the bodily foundation on which man's existence is based. In *The Phenomenological Philosophy of Merleau-Ponty*[3] we

[3] Duquesne University Press, 1963.

began our explanations with an analysis of the "body-subject," the "I-body." For it is important to avoid from the start a misunderstanding that could easily arise if we say that Merleau-Ponty stresses the bodily basis of human existence, viz., a failure to make a distinction between the body-object and the body-subject. Man objectifies reality and among the appearing objects he finds, both in himself and in others, the human body. This body can then be considered as one among many other objects: one can examine, for example, how a plant is constructed, but also how the human body is put together. As other things, man's body is governed by certain laws. A falling rock will crush it, just as it crushes plants and trees; it obeys the laws of gravitation and is vulnerable to cancerous growth as plants and animals are. When Merleau-Ponty wishes to penetrate into the body as the basis of human existence, he is not concerned with this body-object. According to him, the body-object is only a secondary phenomenon because it is the result of a far-reaching abstraction, developed especially by science.

Originally our body is not an object, according to Merleau-Ponty, but lies on the side of the subject. Who am I to whom the world appears and whose life is interwoven with the world? True, I am a thinker, someone who makes free decisions. This we may call our spirit, or rather, the spiritual dimension of our life. But I to whom the world appears am more than this. I am someone who sees, hears, feels, suffers pain, experiences pangs of hunger, is sexualized, speaks and behaves. This I does not coincide with the spiritual dimension of our life. That spiritual dimension is present, but it is not all that I am. My being-subject does not begin with my spiritual dimension. I am a subject even when I feel my feet cramped in shoes that are too small, when I chase away a fly, without even noticing it. I am a subject when I quickly step out of the path of an approaching car, without even knowing how I did it. I am familiar with the world, but I do not owe this familiarity to the spiritual dimension of my life.

My spirit develops and refines a familiarity which was already there. Even on the level of my bodily existence I am familiar with the world, and the way I am familiar with it is difficult to determine by means of reflection. A cook who prepares a delicious meal assumes that the guests are people who like certain things, but she need not know how this relationship of liking has arisen. My body, says Merleau-Ponty, is not locked up in itself, but is an intentionality which in many ways deals with the world and makes the world appear as meaningful reality. It is not the result of any conscious initiative on my part that the world is for me a visual, audible and tactile field, a field of attractive and unattractive things, a field in which there is sexual meaning. As a conscious and free subject, I merely find all this already there as something that arose in the intentional contact between the body-subject and the world.

Merleau-Ponty is convinced that the intentional contact of ourselves as body-subjects with the world is the foundation of our entire intentional life. We are, of course, also conscious and free subjects, but our conscious and free life is a taking up of the bodily life preceding it and can be understood only if this bodily root is taken into account. For the fundamental structures of our life are fixed in this bodily life, in which the fundamental forms of our openness to the world are given. True, we develop this openness in our conscious and free existence, but the latter must be conceived as the unfolding of something pregiven. It is in this sense that Merleau-Ponty's philosophy is a return to the bodily roots of our existence.[4]

[4] "La Pensée ou Conscience est *Offenheit* d'une corporéité à . . . Monde ou Être." *Le visible et l'invisible*, p. 308.

This return, however, cannot be made without great difficulties. Man is sometimes "ungrateful" to the body, in the sense that he lives off it without even noticing it. Thanks to our bodily openness to the world, we are able to interpret the world in an intellectual-spiritual fashion. But it can happen that we consider the result of that interpretation as the original and then try to understand that which really is original in terms of that result. A good example is offered by certain theories of space. Thanks to the body, space is a given to us, so that we are able to form an abstract concept of it. Thus we can arrive at a concept —or should we say a phantasm?—of a single space extending to infinity in all directions, a space that is assumed to be a given reality, in which all things, including our body, are located. Newton formed such a concept of space and thought that the object of this concept was the original reality. In terms of this space one can then proceed to "explain" man's "lived space," i.e., the space which has a foreground, a background and an horizon, a space in which things are in front of me or behind me, high or low, right or left.

This "lived space," it is sometimes said, is only subjective and depends on the particular situation of our body. Subjective and, therefore, unreliable data of this kind should be interpreted and explained in terms of the abstract concept, which alone expresses reality. According to Merleau-Ponty, such a view turns everything upside down. It is the body which makes space appear to me, and the space that appears to me as a body-subject is the original given. All the abstract concepts of space have their origin in the original lived experience of space I have as a body-subject.

Strange as it may seem, our intellectual interpretations can sometimes make us blind to the original given. This is why Merleau-Ponty mistrusts such interpretations and continually attempts to unmask their pseudo-clarity when it conceals primordial givenness. It is to the credit of his philosophical acumen that he often succeeds in this task. Man sometimes has the illusion that he can capture the semi-darkness of life and the world in a clear and distinct synthesis. Combating this illusion, Merleau-Ponty recalls the centuries old reproach addressed to philosophy that "it reverses the roles of the clear and of the obscure."[5] This reproach applies *par excellence* to his own philosophy. The sciences present us with a field of clearly defined objects, but Merleau-Ponty asks us to recognize the derivative character of such a field of thought and to reduce it to a semi-dark field of existence in which everything merges. In experiments man constitutes a transparent world in which interconnections can clearly disclose themselves, but Merleau-Ponty points out that such a laboratory world does not make us understand the authentic field of existence. A distinction is made between physical science and psychology by saying that the former is occupied with the external world and the latter with man's inner world, but Merleau-Ponty denies such a facile distinction between these two worlds. Psychology offers us an orderly whole of concepts through which we acquire a measure of clarity about the complex whole of our inner world, but Merleau-Ponty refers to such an orderly whole as a welter of confusion, a clutter of concepts which we should abandon if we wish to understand anything of ourselves.[6] Generally speaking, Merleau-Ponty's philosophy shows his fear that the light of the constituted may be

[5] *Ibid.*, p. 18.
[6] Cf. *Ibid.*, pp. 209, 277, 289, 307. See our commentary on these texts in *From Phenomenology to Metaphysics*, Duquesne University Press, 1966, pp. 42 f.

a pseudo-light; he therefore tries to withdraw from the constituted to a more original field of existence in which everything is much more in semi-darkness.

3. Aversion for Polished Forms

Starting from this aspect of Merleau-Ponty's philosophy, we can, I think, understand something of what happens in expressive life. Here also there is a movement from light to darkness. Those who are familiar with painters of the past often complain that today's paintings, as compared with those of former times, are dark and confused. Figurative painting offers a picture that is full of clarity, but this clarity has disappeared in the nonfigurative painting that is so popular today. Passing from an exhibition of medieval and renaissance paintings to one of contemporary paintings, one has the feeling of passing from a world of light to a world of darkness. Strange as it seems, however, many people feel attracted by this darkness.

The same phenomenon can be observed when we pay attention to the way children learned to draw between the two world wars and now. Similarly, with respect to sculpture, those who were used to the clarity of the past are shocked by the "monstrosities" which now "disgrace" our parks and public squares. The theater also no longer offers a well-rounded whole, whether it be drama or tragedy, but often merely presents a "happening," without beginning or end, in which the various characters are no longer well integrated, but represent their own inalienable situation. They confront and try to find one another, but sometimes do not succeed. At the end one sometimes does not know what the author of the play wished to say.

The situation is the same in the realm of the novel. Describing the technique of writing a novel in the past,

Sartre says that the novel familiarized us with a life, a period or an event as seen by someone who was not involved in it. Aside from the people described in the novel, there was the person who "witnessed" their lives; the latter was, of course, not described but was the one who made the description. There was a kind of "eternal eye" witnessing temporal events. The look of this eternal eye profoundly affected the development of the temporal events, for it was this watching eye that planned the events.[7] Thus there was a well-rounded whole, with respect to which it was incidental whether it ended on a happy or a sad note. This kind of novel continues to be written even today, but there is also a different kind of novel: the well-rounded whole has vanished, each character is presented as a situation, and it is as if in the novel various human situations struggle with one another to find their way. Unlike formerly, the situations are not described but merely presented, and the characters, as it were, introduce themselves. The reader has no chance to look at a whole through different eyes. Whatever whole there is, is born, as it were, from within, from the presented situations themselves, but there is no guarantee that there will be a whole. The external look on the scene seems to have lost its decisive influence: there is no longer a synthesis. Is the reason perhaps that the novelist feels unable to make a synthesis or is it rather that a synthesis is no longer in harmony with real life? Is the synthesis not a matter of an *a priori* view of life and therefore something which contemporary man views with scepticism?[8]

The same phenomenon also occurs in many contempo-

---

[7] Sartre, "Qu'est-ce que la littérature?", *Situations*, II, Gallimard, Paris, 1948, pp. 177–185.

[8] The synthesis of which there is question here obviously does not refer to the unity of style of a novel, but to the event presented by the book.

rary films, such as *Brief Encounter*, one of the earlier movies of this type. Poetry also is affected by it: people who are familiar with the poetry of the past know how difficult it has become to read contemporary poets.

Let us now take a look at the entertainment world. We find there a new type of music and dance, in which the polished forms of yesteryear have vanished. The older generation intensely dislikes today's music and dancing, which they see sometimes on television: the singing is not polished, there are all kinds of secondary sounds, and some of the notes used would be called false by people accustomed to old-style music. The whole often makes a wild impression, so that some people refer to it as jungle music. The audience, especially if it consists of the younger generation, reacts to the music through body movements, often so violently that it scares those who must maintain order in the hall. This reaction is provoked by the style of the music itself. The latter is not meant for a distinguished audience dressed in tuxedos, but many young people feel quite at home in it.

The contemporary style of dancing corresponds to this kind of music. In a Vienna waltz there is no room for wild movements: clothing and motions are expressions of elegance. In today's dancing the body is not hidden under elegant garments, but its form reveals itself more clearly, and the motion of the body's lower part is more accentuated. The relationship of man and woman is not presented in a refined play of elegant swirls, but much more directly. A former age would have called the modern way of dancing shameless, but that age was also the time when people were ashamed of their bodies. Today's dance is closer to the body—not in the sense that there is no spirit in this dance, but in the sense that the spirit acts much more as an embodied spirit, who is not at all ashamed of being embodied. The body is no longer a stylish instrument of the spirit, but the spirit situates himself in the body, without the former reserve. In short, the body-subject shows itself more than formerly in modern music and dance. The sphere of play remains, of course, but the play is less spiritualized than formerly.

It will not do to dismiss these novel ways of making music and dancing by saying that they are followed by people who are not really artistic, that we live in a world of superficial entertainment and not in an era of genuine art. In these modern forms of music and dance also there are prominent specialists, who have reached the top only through much practice and perseverance. They may impress the spectator or listener by the apparently casual ease of their performance, but this ease often is based on long and continuous training. One does not cheaply reach prominence in the modern entertainment world or on television, but has to survive a merciless critical review of one's performance. Society at large may be "stupid," but it is not so stupid that it gives millions of dollars to mediocrities. True, "stars" are sometimes artificially cultivated, they may shine brilliantly but ephemerally like a pyrotechnic display, but that is not all that can be said about the modern world of entertainment. It will not do simply to claim that the taste of the younger generation is spoiled by today's producers of records and television shows. Although there may be a grain of truth in this claim, much more important is the fact that the younger generation itself positively wishes to have a different way of making music and dancing and no longer feels at home in the polished world of yesteryear.

All this is in line with a movement manifesting itself in education. In former times it was assumed that there existed fixed forms of life and therefore the younger generation was introduced to these existing forms. They learned to draw by reproducing fixed models, to write by copying letters exactly according to model, and in every respect they were introduced to established forms of expression. Today, however, they are given more leeway, they have an opportunity for free expression. They are given a sheet of drawing paper and told to fill it according to their own initiative. Obviously, the idea is not to leave everything at that, there is no wish to abandon the wealth of the past and let everyone for himself discover again the techniques of drawing. After a period of free expression, an appeal is made to the wealth of the past. Room is left, nevertheless, for free expression. The students are invited to find their own way, and the teachers are not afraid of "wild" results. It can be interesting today to visit a show of children's drawings.

It stands to reason that today's expressive life does not show a rectilinear development. There are movements and countermovements, and a style that disappears can again return to the scene. Besides, as much as possible, we try to preserve the past in our museums, where one can become acquainted with the way man has painted and sculptured in many periods. In our histories of art we study the development of expressive life throughout the whole of recorded history. Expert art historians can date works of art with the greatest of ease. We organize, moreover, festivals of art, during which performers imitate the expressive life of the past. Finally, increased international contacts quickly make things that appear important known all over the world. One who becomes an authority in some field can expect invitations for lectures to reach him from the most diverse parts of the world.

Because we preserve in this way the past and become familiar with what is far away, we less easily become encapsulated in a fixed system of expressive forms. There is more variation than formerly, and the changes occur much more rapidly. The danger is not at all imaginary that we know too much to be "ourselves" in our expression. Today it is difficult to speak of a general direction of expressive life, and to this must be added that today's expressive life is still evolving and that we ourselves take part in it. In other words, it is only in a very relative sense that one can speak of a general movement or direction in our expressive life. There is no universal acceptance of the general movement and there are also countercurrents. Besides, many people do not take part in it. In spite of all this, however, it is possible to discern a general line in today's expressive life.

There exist a certain aversion for the polished forms of former times, the well-rounded synthesis in drama and novel, the refined ways of dancing, the kind of music that perfectly fitted in with the stately music hall. It is as if people today find those forms of expression too "spiritualized," that is, they expressed a way of being-a-spirit which tries to keep aloof from the body, a way in which the body does not clearly play its part. An unambiguous example of what is meant here is the way of thinking criticized by Merleau-Ponty. One thinks in a scientifically purified way and through this way of thinking constructs a neatly ordered field of thought; then, one tries to interpret the lived world in terms of this mental construct. Merleau-Ponty protests against this kind of thinking because it makes people interpret the real world in terms of an intellectual abstraction which may be clear but, at the same time, also presents only a one-sided picture. He thinks that we should return to the lived world, which is more obscure but, at the same time, much richer, albeit that its wealth is latent. For this reason he often uses the expression "savage Being" in his last work.[9] In "savage

[9] The same term occurs already in some articles incorporated in his book *Signs*, but those articles were written relatively close to his writing of his last book.

Being" everything is still "scrambled," everything is still permeated with everything else. There is not yet the neat order of reason. That neat order is a valuable but one-sided abstraction from the "wild" world in which real life runs its course.

It should be clear now that, with respect to expressive life, many contemporaries are not solely opposed to the dictatorship of science and technology. Science and technology are exponents of a more general phenomenon, viz., a world that is polished in every respect. That polished world, which revealed itself in literature, sculpture, painting, music, dance and even recreational activities, can still provoke the admiration of contemporary man, but he no longer believes in it, he can no longer see that world as our real world. It is not impossible that the existence of that polished world was connected with the fact that formerly culture was something pertaining to the privileged few, something realized by an elite and accessible only to an elite. It is not improbable that by constructing such a polished world in man's forms of expression, this elite wished to express their own lofty situation above "ordinary" people. Today, however, we live in an era of more widespread culture. True, it is obviously still the elite few who are creative of culture, but they no longer work only for the privileged few: they now address themselves to the public at large. Thus it is unavoidable that our forms of expression now reveal the attitudes of the many rather than the few.

Now, it is undeniable that everywhere one can observe an aversion for the above-mentioned polished world and a turning to a "wilder" world in which the body, as our gate to the world, plays a greater role. The polished world of yesteryear was the world of the transcended and, therefore, also somewhat forgotten body. Today's generation is no longer "ashamed" of the body, and its men of letters do not hesitate to refer to the body in terms which formerly were heard only in slums and taverns. Everything pertaining to concrete life now finds expression. Our contemporaries see nothing objectionable in being absorbed by the body while listening to music or dancing, and this manifests itself in the style of today's music and dance. The spirit continues to play its orderly role, of course, for otherwise there could be no question of contemporary culture. But this spirit openly recognizes that it is the spirit of a body and that, in its creation of order, it takes up something that is given with the body-subject. This spirit realizes that it no longer knows everything and does not even feel any need to know everything. As creative of order, the spirit situates itself in the rhythm of man's bodily existence, it takes up this rhythm and creates order in terms of this rhythm. No longer is everything expressed in ways that are justified in terms of the spirit. People express themselves in this or that way because they are this way or that way, without knowing why they are this way or that way. There are thinkers who view all this as alarming symptoms of the threatening decline of our culture, but those who really accept man as an embodied spirit view all this as a form of culture which is exactly suited to man.

How widespread this new form of culture is becomes evident when we consider what is happening in countries behind the iron curtain. The leaders of those countries favored scientific socialism and therefore formulated a cultural policy which fostered forms of expression that fitted in with the existence planned by scientific socialism. These forms had to be polished but different, of course, from those prevailing among the capitalistic classes that ruled elsewhere. The theater and the novel had to be governed by socialistic realism, as is exemplified by the fixed pattern of the novels written during the Stalinistic period. The wild music and dances of the West did not fit in with the socialistic ideas of recreational activities and were therefore characterized as clear signs of the West's decadence and heralds of its impending doom. Paintings were universally dull because the artists had to follow the established patterns if they did not wish to fall from grace. Strange as it seems, in spite of the fact that these countries called themselves materialistic, the revolutionary order demanded that all expression be exceedingly spiritualistic, that is, it imposed an intellectual system in which there was no room for the many aspects found in man's embodied existence.

The entire new generation was educated in such a sphere, in which expressive life fell under the dictatorship of rational knowledge. Attempts were made to close the door to influences from without. Nevertheless, the wild Western forms of expression have managed to penetrate those countries and it has become evident that even there they evoked a spontaneous response and acceptance among the younger generation. The cultural policy of the socialistic state proved unable to resist the pressure, so that at present we find in the U.S.S.R. and its satellites on a rather widespread scale the expressive phenomena with which we are familiar in the West. This fact is all the more striking because these forms of expression are not fostered there, as they are in the West, by commercial interests. We may see in this an indication that these phenomena point to a rather general contemporary attitude.

We do not mention here underdeveloped countries where modern science is not yet pursued as vigorously as in Western Europe and America, where technology is still in its infancy and there is not yet any modern generalized order of work. In such countries man's bodily being probably has not been forgotten in man's attempts to self-transcendence, so that there is no need to regain a "wildness" which has never been lost there. In those countries the above-mentioned situation does not occur, but we find it again in Japan, a country that has shared in the development of the West.

There is another fact that must be mentioned here, viz., the return to manual labor. It figures sometimes as a course on the program of secondary schools under the name of handicrafts. Manual labor has gone through a strange history of development. For many centuries—one could say from the beginning of mankind to the modern period—manual labor was an inexorable and hard necessity. Man had to wrest his living from the earth through work, and the first source of the needed energy he found in his own body. It is no coincidence that the term "labor" can mean both work and travail.[10] The weariness of the necessary effort has for centuries overshadowed the joy which accompanies all expression, so that work could sometimes be viewed as something to which man was doomed. Unsurprisingly, the toilsome working with one's hands became the lot of those who were socially or economically weak and a task from which the "better" classes tried to exempt themselves. Manual labor was for slaves, serfs and other low-ranking members of society. In Plato's proposed social order the workers occupied the lowest place.[11]

In recent times, however, man has discovered a way to liberate himself from laboriously working with his hands, by letting machines do this kind of work for him. Instead

[10] Hannah Arendt, in her book *The Human Condition*, University of Chicago Press, 1958, has a chapter entitled "Labor," pp. 79–135. She there approaches the phenomenon of labor in terms of the ancient meanings of the Latin *labor* and its English derivative. It does not seem to us that this is the proper approach to an understanding of modern labor.

[11] See his *Republic*, bk. IX.

of exhausting his bodily strength by digging a deep ditch with a simple spade, he now lets a mechanical ditch-digger do such heavy work, which a few decades ago was still done by hand. In examples of this kind one can see what liberation from manual labor means. The younger generation is becoming so accustomed to this freedom that they hardly realize in what toilsome ways their fathers had to work.

In the modern process of work many people barely need to use their hands. They observe and control a process started by man but which runs its course automatically. Through cybernetics even this control will become less and less necessary. Now that work begins to need man less, however, there arises in man a need to work with his hands—not as a necessity but as a form of spending his leisure hours. Man begins to work again with his hands for the simple reason that he likes doing this. It is no longer work in the strict sense of the term, as making provisions for his bodily needs, but a matter of recreation. He makes something simply because he likes making things and does not mind the effort involved. In former times he had to expend his bodily energy in his work and he then experienced this need as a burden. Now, however, the expenditure of bodily energy is hardly needed in many forms of work, leaving man, as it were, with a surplus of energy to be disposed of in his leisure hours. Thus he looks for things to do with his hands, work that demands bodily effort. One could say he likes to perspire again now that he no longer needs to work "in the sweat of his brow."

Modern labor is guided by the light of science and has largely outgrown the dimensions of the body. In former times work took place in a world that was literally manipulable, for it was done with the hands. The entire world of work referred to the body's dimensions, as is still the case with such things as a motorcycle or car, which are guided by man's hands and feet. This is no longer the case in the most modern sectors of our world of labor. There we find now a giant production apparatus whose workings are not obvious and which indicates by light signals whether or not it is functioning properly. For the ordinary citizen such an apparatus is a kind of a "black box": he sees what goes into it and comes out of it, but what happens inside escapes him. While at present this kind of production apparatus is not yet general, increasingly more sections of the world of work are being taken over by it. It is for this reason that we can say that work is now outgrowing the dimensions of the human body, the body is becoming "unemployed."

If in former times man complained that too much was demanded of his bodily energy, today he appears even less inclined to accept the "unemployed" condition of his body. The latter, moreover, is harmful to his health. Paradoxical as it is, man now seeks again that from which he had liberated himself only a short while ago. He seeks it, however, within a new context, not that of work but of leisure. Manual skills are now being taught even in schools that are not trade schools in the traditional sense of the term; clubs are founded for the pursuit of such skills, and in the cities hobby shops are becoming popular.

Here also, then, there occurs a return to the dimensions of the body in the development of expressive life. Man is a self-transcending movement, and often his self-transcendence implies a spiritualization of life and the world. With the aid of scientific understanding man builds for himself a world which transcends the dimensions of his body. He does this not only in the above-mentioned world of work but also in the sphere of communication. We have contact with one another far beyond the reach of our eyes or the distance our voice can carry. The systems of providing for our needs likewise exceed our bodily reach: what we need is no longer delivered by hand to our door, but often reaches us through wires, pipes and invisible waves in the form of water, heat, cooled air, and electric energy. We live in a world that has been organized by man's rationality and which therefore transcends the dimensions of our bodies. Because of this world, we can live in greater comfort and feel less threatened in our existence. At the same time, however, there exists also in many respects a movement in the opposite direction: we feel a need for a world adapted to the dimensions of our body, for our body is our primordial gateway to the world. No one, of course, wishes to undo what man has achieved; on the contrary, man's conquest and control of nature should continue. But we return in a different way to the body which we have transcended: we build within the macro-world a micro-world that is adapted to our body.

4. Conclusion

In this chapter we have tried to indicate a general direction in the development of man's expressive life. This direction lies, we think, in a return to the dimensions of man's bodily existence. Expressive life tries to be in harmony with the life rhythm of the body. Our existence does not run its course in a scientific field of thought, and this makes modern man look again for the original dimensions, from which also the scientific field of thought was born. The polished cultural world of yesteryear's elite tired and bored us: it was so polished that it could not give expression to all kinds of forces that are at work in man. There arises a "wilder" cultural world in which the younger generation feels more at home. We have spiritualized our workaday world so much that we feel the need for something in which we are again bodily involved in an "ordinary" way. Walking or cycling becomes again popular now that we have motorized transportation. People now like to go to mountain regions for recreational purposes, though in past centuries mountains were largely pure obstacles. Opportunities are created for handicrafts and forms of work that are not "needed." At school, children are asked to draw or paint according to their own inspiration, instead of being forced to copy fixed models, because otherwise their nascent expressivity could become too channelized. Attempts are made to draw the whole body into expressivity, so that one no longer speaks only with one's voice but with the whole face and with hands and feet. There is no longer any desire to lock the body up in a high level spiritual culture, but the body itself must be free.

Does not all this contain a danger of lapsing into primitivism? It must undoubtedly be admitted that this danger exists and that there are alarming phenomena. There is every reason to rejoice when the younger generation likes to listen to music, or rather, likes to live music and manifests this by bodily motions. Throughout history the rhythm of music has always made itself felt in the body and provoked the body to motion; hence it is not at all obvious that music should be quietly listened to. But, it is not a cause for satisfaction when large numbers of policemen are needed to preserve order and prevent the hall from being wrecked when many young people attend. While it may be all to the good that today's younger generation does not wish to live in the polished world of yesteryear's cultural elite, this wish does not justify their sometimes strangely provocative attitude. Merleau-Ponty emphasized a valuable point when he spoke of "savage Being," for, relatively to the more or less somnolent quiet of the past, modern man needs more "wildness." Yet, this wildness may not degenerate into a nihilistic attitude with respect to the past.

In the past development of his existence man often transcended its bodily basis so much that the body did not receive its due. With its many-sided possibilities it was often compressed into too narrow a framework. Culture exists, of course, thanks to the human spirit, so that it would be folly to turn against the spirit. But it is not excluded that the spirit organizes a cultural world which becomes a prison for the bodily dimension of man's existence. As a matter of fact, it would be difficult to deny that this has often occurred in the past generations. Our schools were so intent on the spirit that the children seemed to have only brains. Hands and feet and a body that needs movement appeared to be unknown to the educators of the time, so that the pupils' bodily existence did not receive its due. Entire sections of cities were built in such a way that those living there did not have any chance to realize their powers of expression: no room for playing or sports, recreation, the pursuit of hobbies or artistic endeavors. Everything was built in terms of the absolute minimum requirements of space for sleeping, sitting down and eating, thus dooming the inhabitants to a purely utilitarian and monotonous existence. Today, thanks to our increased productivity, we have been freed from all kinds of needs, we have more time to devote to all kinds of expression. Unfortunately, however, our world is not yet sufficiently attuned to this increased leisure, it is still largely built for people who do not possess that freedom.

In the development of expressive life, we said, there occurs a return to the bodily basis of our existence, and this return contains a danger of primitivism. The presence of this danger, however, may not induce us to pronounce a negative judgment on this development. In our opinion, there is much in this development that has a positive value. It rectifies much of the one-sidedness characteristic of the past, it tears down walls of the prison in which we too often used to lock up our bodily existence. In the development of his human existence man does not have any other starting point than his bodily being, and his bodily existence remains the foundation of the entire development. This foundation contains many possibilities, but they are there in a latent form only. In former times this bodily basis was often utilized much too one-sidedly, disregarding some of man's bodily possibilities. In this sense we may say that in the past man had a "forgotten body." Unsurprisingly, this forgotten body finally protested, and we now try to give it its due. There are obvious dangers in this attempt, but nonetheless the attempt itself is good.

Our era is a difficult time for overall views of life. Such views always endeavor to present a total picture of human existence. In the past, even the recent past, it was much easier to present such a total view, but today life presents new aspects and, in particular, we try to find new ways of expression. Life has become "wilder" and it is more difficult now to establish order. Because we have seen so many of the past overall views of life unmasked as one-sided, we now hesitate to present an overall view, for we realize that such a view can unduly restrict human existence. We live in an era of confusion but, strange as it seems, many people are far from unhappy over this: they prefer the liberating confusion to the unduly restrictive order. Is this confusion merely a result of living in a period of transition or is it a permanent phenomenon? The author must confess that he is unable to answer this question.

CHAPTER SEVEN

Religious Expression

1. THE PROBLEM OF RELIGIOUS EXPRESSION

IT MAY BE useful to devote special attention to one particular form of expression, viz. the religious expression.
Travelling through the older areas of Europe's cities, one
finds himself surrounded by religious expression in many
forms. We say "the older areas," for in this respect there
is a striking difference between many of the old cores and
the newer sections. In the old cores one usually finds
everywhere monuments of religious expression, to such an
extent that if all of them were removed from the streets,
parks and museums, an essential ingredient of these cores
would disappear. This situation does not exist, however,
in the new sections. True, these sections contain
churches and in these churches there are works of religious art, but one cannot say that removing the churches
and their art would cut the heart out of these areas, at
least with respect to their external appearance. It is as if in
former times the forms of religious expression dominated
the humanized world, the world which man made his by
expressing himself in it. Today one can no longer say the
same.

Moreover, if we compare the past forms of religious
expression with those of today, it seems that man has

become more hesitant and less certain of himself. In the past we find styles of religious expression which managed to prevail for a century or even longer in man's way of building, painting or sculpturing; for instance, the roman, the gothic or the baroque forms of architecture. Even in the past, of course, there was a certain amount of seeking and groping for expression, but it occurred within fixed styles that were more or less firmly adhered to. In the recent past, man at first imitated these established styles, he built neo-gothic, neo-roman or neo-baroque churches. Today, however, he is tired of such imitations and tries to find his own form of religious expression. He strikes out in all directions, sometimes with considerable success, but it is difficult to recognize a common pattern in today's attempts. The same kind of searching and groping can be observed when one visits an exhibition of contemporary religious painting or sculpture. We have become more hesitant and less certain of ourselves in our religious expression.

Let us add that today it has become very difficult to speak of religious expression. Organizers of exhibitions experience great difficulty in trying to determine what is and what is not religious art. And when they make a choice, they can be certain that many will object and criticize it. The difficulty is not merely practical but also theoretical: it has become almost impossible to state in theory what religious art is.[1] We no longer seem to know what religious expression is.

It would be wrong, however, to assert that in former ages the concept of religious expression and its distinction from nonreligious expression were perfectly clear. Part of that alleged clarity was merely pseudo-clarity. If, for ex-

---

[1] See, e.g., the March, 1958, issue of *Kunst en religie*, which contains a series of lectures about the concept "religious art." They eloquently illustrate the above-mentioned difficulty.

ample, we visit the museums of Florence, where many of Botticelli's paintings are preserved, we can see there his famous Madonnas side by side with his Venus. The former have a religious topic, the latter does not, but the style remains fundamentally the same. If, then, we consider his Madonnas works of religious art, we should do the same for his Venus, and vice versa. The same remark could be made about the works of Rubens and many other painters. The historical reasons are well known: those painters received a commission from patrons and had to paint the topics selected by them, regardless of whether they themselves felt any inner urge to produce religious art.

If we wish to make a distinction between religious and nonreligious art, we cannot use the represented topic as a decisive criterion. By the same token, however, the alleged clarity of former ages disappears into thin air. Both in the present and in the past it is difficult to make a distinction between religious art and other forms of art.

The same difficulty is experienced when we devote our attention to other forms of expression. One cannot say, for example, that the gothic style is a religious style, for not only churches but many other buildings of the same period were constructed in the same style. Similarly, in the Middle Ages, theology was often called "sacred," for the avowed purpose of indicating that theology is a scientific —in the medieval sense—way of speaking born from a religious inspiration. In other words, theology was a religious expression. If, however, one reads certain medieval treatises of theology, he experiences that God and things divine are approached in an attitude of mind and in a style which are exactly the same as those used for nonreligious matters. Even in the Middle Ages there were people who protested against the lack of "sacredness" in "sacred theology" and condemned it as mere pseudo-sacredness. In other words, it does not solely depend on the topic whether our speaking is religious or not. We encounter this same difficulty in every field of so-called religious expression.

2. CLARITY AND MYSTERY

What are we to understand by the religious dimension of life? Strange as it seems, there are people today who do not believe in God but who, nonetheless, recognize man's religious dimension. In several respects this fact can serve to clarify matters. To a certain extent man lives in a field of clarity, both in the theoretical and in the practical order. Let us first look at the practical order. We would be unable to act if the things of the world handled by us did not have a clear meaning for us. For one who types, the machine's function is clear and he knows what he is supposed to do with the paper. The driver of a car must know his vehicle and be familiar with traffic signs. The skilled worker knows exactly what he can do with his instruments and materials. Each one is familiar with the things in his home. Heidegger refers to the field of manipulable things as a "totality of involvements" consisting of things that are "ready to hand."[2] This totality is, as it were, a familiar extension of ourselves. In short, we live in a field of clarity; otherwise we could not even live. Practical life offers problems, of course, but we are able to deal with those problems because many things present no problems to us.

Clarity exists not only in the field of action but also in that of speech. In our everyday language there are many things which everyone accepts unquestionedly, for we can converse with one another only if we have commonly accepted things. The names, for example, which we give to things are common, and the same must be said of many judgments we make. Our language is intentional, that is,

[2] "Bewanntnisganzheit." Cf. *Sein und Zeit*, pp. 83–88.

it verbally expresses the reality in and around us. Our speaking helps to make us familiar with our world and ourselves. Thanks to the unquestionedly accepted things of our common speech, we live in a field of clarity. Even where human speech remains primitive, it offers clarity, no matter how primitive this field of clarity may be.

Through the sciences and the resulting technology, modern man has greatly developed his field of clarity. We are just as familiar with electric light and television as primitive man was with his primitive tools. Let us add that this clarity about our world coincides with the clarity we have about the way we must act and speak in this world. We would not be familiar with the manipulable world if we were not familiar also with our body as manipulating the world. The experienced driver can quickly and unhesitatingly execute the actions through which his body manipulates his car.

When, however, we reflect upon our field of clarity, we realize that it has a horizon of darkness. No scientific, philosophical or religious reflection is needed to make this discovery. Primitive man also was aware of this darkness. Man experiences that his field of clarity has limits and he knows that limits will remain even if he manages to extend his field of clarity. Moreover, and this is even more important, our field of clarity leads a threatened existence. It can collapse, for it is essentially connected with the possibilities of our bodily existence, with our possibilities of speaking and acting. These possibilities are threatened from within. From time to time anyone experiences these threats. One who feels the first signs of a weakening of the heart is frightened because his whole existence is threatened. Our entire field of existence leads a threatened life. This is also the reason why people extend their good wishes to one another: such wishes would be meaningless if our field of existence consisted solely of unthreatened certainties. On going to bed, we do not express the wish that the sun may rise again tomorrow, though we may wish that its rise will be unclouded.

Man is origin and source of meaning, but not in an absolute way. He knows that in his being-a-source he is dependent. We are dependent in everything upon our body, with which, on the one hand, we are familiar because we know how to work and act with it, and which, on the other, we do not need to know in the full sense of the term. Most people, for example, see, without knowing how the eye works; everyone thinks, but there is no one who fully knows how our brain operates. Similarly, we are familiar with the manipulable world, without fully knowing what matter is or what the world is. No one has ever managed to give a satisfactory definition of the world, yet we can live in it. In all our projects we make use of given possibilities. It is, says Merleau-Ponty, as if there exists a "pre-established harmony" (Leibniz) between our bodily existence and the world.[3] These two are attuned to each other, and every new success in our fruitful "metabolism" (Marx) with the world is a new proof of the fact that they are attuned to each other. Our eye and the world are such that their encounter gives rise to our visible field, and the encounter of our rational acting with the world gives birth to the technical field of existence.

If we reflect upon the lucid field in which life runs its course, we encounter a horizon of darkness at the root of our clarity. The term "horizon" is not very suitable, however; it would be better to say that darkness surrounds our field of light, or that darkness is present in the depth of our field of existence. For in our search for ground we

[3] "Le regard, disions-nous, enveloppe, palpe, épouse les choses visibles. Comme s'il était avec elles dans un rapport d'harmonie préétablie, comme s'il les savait avant de les savoir, il bouge à sa façon dans son style saccadé et impérieux, et pourtant les vues prises ne sont pas quelconques, je ne regarde pas un chaos, mais des choses, de sorte qu'on ne peut pas dire enfin si c'est lui ou si c'est elles qui commandent." *Le visible et l'invisible*, p. 175.

encounter darkness. Whether we speak, however, of horizon, surroundings or depth, we are using quantitative images for something which is not quantitative. Anyone who thinks authentically must recognize that, living in a field of clarity, we encounter darkness in the depth of this field. This statement applies also to the Marxist view of life, which states that matter in dialectic evolution is the origin of everything. The Marxists use certain words to indicate this origin: they speak of matter which is in dialectic development, in such a way that at a given moment a quantitative complexity brings about a qualitative change. Such an assertion consists of words which, properly understood, merely point into darkness. The assertion is a hypothesis which, insofar as it is adhered to as certain, assumes the character of being an act of faith. Areligious humanism also recognizes this horizon of darkness, and the followers of areligious humanism are willing to speak of a mystery in this matter.

Now, the religious view of life occupies itself with this mysterious dimension. All religions are concerned with it. Religion is a consciousness of Origin, it is an affirmation concerned with the above-mentioned obscure dimension, and this affirmation has the character of an act of faith. An expression is religious when man expresses himself in terms of this dimension.[4]

It stands to reason that man wishes to occupy himself with this dimension of Origin. One can wonder about an unusual combination of phenomena, such as a two-headed calf, but our wonder can also be concerned with the existence of phenomena as such, of ourselves and our world. Why is it that we are, that we are as we are, that we find ourselves in a world, that the world is adapted to us and we to the world? Man does not stop with any question whatsoever, but in his reflection continues to raise further

[4] This self-expression can occur even when one does not have a theory about the religious dimension of man.

questions. He makes one phenomenon intelligible in terms of another. Expanding his field of clarity, he increasingly suspects that there is a universal connection of everything. The Greeks therefore used the term "cosmos," which means both order and world. Our knowing itself is contained within this connection and forms a part of it.

Merleau-Ponty was very much aware of this universal interconnection during the last period of his life and therefore continually used the expression "I belong to it." I am a fragment of visible reality which becomes a seeing of all visible reality, I am a piece of reality that can be reflected upon and which becomes a reflection upon all reality. All our acting and all our knowing takes place within the interconnection of everything with everything else and we therefore rightly suspect that there is a universal interconnection, although we are unable to comprehend this universal interconnection. We have words to affirm it, e.g., we use the Greek *cosmos*, the Latin *universum*, and our own *world*. But, because we ourselves form part of this universal interconnection, we can never exactly define the meaning of those terms. The universal interconnection of everything can never be scientifically verified because any such verification itself is encompassed by the interconnection. True, any new discovery of an interconnection is a new reference to the universal interconnection, but we can never bring the universal interconnection's discovery to a close. Must we say, then, that our affirmation of this universal bond is an irrational act of faith? In the author's opinion, this is not the case. Our affirmation aims at something which manifests itself in everything but which, at the same time, transcends everything; we affirm something which becomes visible in everything, but which can never be isolated as an object.

The religious man is convinced that this universal interconnection of everything with everything else does not have its ground in itself and that it cannot ultimately be understood solely in terms of itself. He, therefore, believes in an Origin, which is traditionally referred to as "God." There is question here of an act of faith because in our affirmation of God as Origin we are concerned with something that is in principle not subject to verification. The term "cause" also is used in this matter, but receives here a very special meaning. We are familiar with the cause and effect relationship and when we affirm this relationship in the ordinary field of existence, we affirm a connection between two known realities. In the sphere of the religious affirmation, however, we affirm a connection of known reality with an Origin which we do not directly know and which we will never be able to verify. Whether or not the affirmation of God is justified is a question pertaining to metaphysics; it need not concern us here in this chapter devoted to religious expression.

3. RECOGNITION OF DARKNESS AND AFFIRMATION OF LIGHT

We would like to distinguish two fundamental spheres of religious expression. First, it is possible that reflective man comes to the realization that our field of existence is permeated with a dimension of darkness. Secondly, man can "fill" this darkness by means of his religious affirmation. One could say that in the first case man penetrates into a fundamental question and that, in the second, he gives expression to his belief in an answer.[5]

[5] This distinction manifests itself very clearly in Kant's philosophy. Kant critically investigated the possibilities of theoretical reason to affirm reality and arrived at the conclusion that, left to itself, theoretical reason is unable to make affirmations concerning God. Theoretical reason, however, is not the highest function of man. Practical reason is more important because it serves a higher goal. Hence theoretical reason must recognize the postulates of practical reason. Now, the affirmation of God is such a postulate. The affirmation of God, then, ultimately is for Kant an affirmation without theoretical insight.

Near Central Park Ave.

SALE

奈 良

Cold duck

Two ducks take off from Lake Cornelia in Edina, Minn.
The other ducks seem to be frozen immobile as tempera-

hit 5 below zero. Warmer temperatures are forecast
Midwest on Saturday. (AP)

Let us begin by paying attention to the recognition of the dimension of darkness. By recognizing this darkness, man recognizes the contingency, the inconsistency of the light and clarity given to him. He does not deny this light and this clarity, but he denies that they have their ground in themselves. He thus rejects the unquestionableness of the unquestionedly accepted light, he begins to wonder and is astonished that there is light, that there is connection, order, that there is a "cosmos." He begins to realize that all this arises from the fact that man goes to the encounter of reality as a manifold question and that he constitutes reality as an answer to the question which he is. Man, however, *finds* himself as a manifold question, and he *finds* reality as something that can become an answer, a meaning for him. Once man realizes this, all light is indeed permeated with darkness. Man's consciousness of this darkness is not taken away by the fact that he finally finds more light. On the contrary, the discovery of more light increases his wonder. Every new development of science, every new technological achievement offers new material for this fundamental wonder. This wonder is not a question lying in the same line as the ordinary questions of science, but it is concerned with something that is also the foundation of all scientific questions and answers. This wonder implies that man recognizes the fact that the entire edifice of his knowledge and power does not offer him what he ultimately seeks. For the entire edifice is based on suppositions and, as such, its existence is a threatened and contingent existence.[6]

It would be wrong to assume that only the philosopher can penetrate into the darkness with which all light is permeated. This darkness is acknowledged in literature, poetry and other forms of contemporary art. Generally

[6] This idea is clearly expressed in Merleau-Ponty's little work, *In Praise of Philosophy*, Northwestern University Press, 1963. This work contains his inaugural lecture at the *Collège de France*.

speaking, representatives of modern art do not exactly share the view of "technological optimism," i.e., the optimistic view that modern man can develop his world without running into any fundamental problems. In today's art one continually encounters the question of what meaning this world has. Contemporary art generally does not offer us a clear, obvious and transparent world, but draws attention to the chaotic dimension permeating our world. It remains true, of course, that today's painters, like their predecessors, wish to conjure up before our eyes the core, the essence of the visible world. We use here the term "conjure" because the metamorphosis of the given visible field into a painting is not a rational process. The painter does not know with rational clarity what he is doing or why he is doing it as he does. And when he begins to theorize about his intentions, he can easily be mistaken about himself, for his intentions are not endowed with a rigorous rationality. Now, when today's painters visualize the world, they often present us with something chaotic. Paradoxically expressed, one could say that they emphasize the dark aspects of our modern world of light. In this matter there exists a great difference between contemporary paintings and those of the Renaissance. The latter generally offer us a clear world of light, an orderly world. It is as if they wish to tell us that the core of the visible world is order, clarity and transparency. It suffices to look at the paintings of Perugino, Rafael and Botticelli. One could even speak of a tendency to idealize the world in this respect. Today's painters, however, seem no longer to believe that order, clarity and transparency are the ultimate truth about our world. They seem to view light, order and clarity as a superficial illusion which conceals the reality of darkness. This is all the more remarkable because, more than ever before, contemporary man is a builder of his own world.

The same phenomenon occurs in contemporary poetry. The clarity of the traditional forms of poetry is largely gone. The clear and smooth verse seems to impress our poets today as something mendacious, something that is not in agreement with the reality of modern existence. One could even say that today's poetry is characterized by a kind of disorder, albeit an "orderly" kind of disorder. Form and content are no longer separable. The "wildness" of today's poetry is an indication that the contemporary poet discovers darkness in our reputedly clear world. Again, it is not a question of a denial that there is light, but of discovering that this light has a fundamental dimension of darkness.

What has all this to do with religious expression? The answer is that it lays bare the dimension with which the religious affirmation is, and always has been, concerned. It very often happens that this dimension is laid bare without being "filled" with a religious affirmation. Many artists assume a negative attitude toward the religious affirmation, but this does not mean that they are not occupied with the same dimension in which the religious affirmation moves. In such a case they do not attain confidence and hope, but end up with hopelessness, anxiety, despair and a feeling that life is meaningless. The void or emptiness then seems to become the ultimate truth of life. The situation is not without paradox. In many respects religion goes through a crisis today, yet more than ever people enter the dimension in which religion moves. Even of Russian art it is true that today it goes in this same direction and that to a large extent it has broken with socialistic optimism. Many Russian artists no longer believe in the revolutionary creed that the capitalistic period of estrangement will be followed by a world which is human without any qualification. The religious dimension fascinates man, even when he has become religionless.

The recognition of darkness remains connected with the religious dimension, even when man has become religionless.

There is a striking resemblance between the orientation of many contemporary artists and a philosophy like that of Merleau-Ponty. This philosopher can hardly be called a thinker who develops our world of light, who studies technology, the logic of light-producing thought. On the contrary, he constantly endeavors to point to the dark roots of the light in which we live and the reality of which he does not at all deny. In the first phase of his philosophical development—which centers around PHENOMENOLOGY OF PERCEPTION—he viewed the contingent dialog between the human subject and the world as the source of all meaning, all light. The "top" of this dialog is free and conscious, and therefore full of light, but its foundation lies in the semidarkness of embodied existence, in which reflection can penetrate only with the greatest difficulty. In the second phase of his philosophical development—that of THE VISIBLE AND THE INVISIBLE— Merleau-Ponty views the dialog between man and world as an intentional dualization. This expression indicates that reality, Being, comes to be in man as a seeing, feeling, tasting, thinking and speaking of itself. There is a dualization because the original unity, as it were, doubles itself into subject and object. By virtue of this intentional dualization reality becomes accessible to itself. Reality, however, must always be seen in the light of the original unity, or rather in the darkness of this unity, for the original unity is not accessible in itself. This kind of thinking is a philosophy of the constituted, the nonoriginal, the ever-contingent and threatened character of the light, it is a philosophy which warns us that we should never forget that all light is rooted in darkness and always remains permeated with obscurity. One could say that contemporary artists in their own way give expression to the same idea through the obscurity of their verse and the orderly disorder of their paintings and sculptures.

Philosophy and art are expressions of an existential experience. We mean that modern man experiences how profoundly hidden in obscurity his roots are, how contingent and exposed to danger his existence is. Contemporary man is very much aware of all this, but one cannot say that in former times this experience was entirely foreign to man. The experience in question undoubtedly is more widespread today because, being able to look deeper into history and social structures, we are more conscious than our ancestors were of the historical and social facticity of our existence. In former times when a given situation *de facto* seemed to be changeless, man could easily think that this situation was necessary and immutable. Today, however, we know that our human situation—including our scientific knowledge and technical power—is the fruit of a long and common attempt of man to situate himself and that, therefore, it is mutable and contingent. Although man is now more powerful than formerly, he knows that his power is rooted in powerlessness.

When this consciousness finds expression, we may speak of "religious expression" because it puts the accent on the dimension in which there is room for the affirmation of God. The mere recognition of this dimension does not mean, of course, the affirmation of God. On the contrary, there are many people who recognize this dimension and still deny God's existence. Nevertheless, there is a connection between this dimension and the affirmation of God.

The religious man, we said above, "fills" this dimension with his affirmation of God. He believes that ultimately this dimension is not nothing. Man's affirmation of this dimension implies that his reflection extends to this di-

171

mension, that the phenomenal field of light is not the final and ultimate dimension of reality because he experiences that the field of light itself is rooted and contingent. For the religious man the dark roots of the region of light imply an Origin endowed with a personal character, which is at work in everything and pervades man and the world. The religious man calls this Origin "God."

In this way there arises a new sphere of religious expression, of which prayer is the foremost form. Believing in a personal Origin of everything, the religious man will speak to God.[7] Man's speaking sometimes assumes the form of song and is accompanied by gestures: the same can happen to religious expression. The believer in God also believes that God works in him and makes Himself known to him. He realizes that he cannot affirm God without affirming, at the same time, that God makes Himself known to him. He knows that God is at work in his own consciousness of Origin. This consciousness of Origin is stronger in some people than in others, and it can assume a very striking form in those who become founders of a religion. The latter function with respect to their fellowmen as witnesses to their consciousness of Origin, of God. A term that is often used in this connection is that of "revelation," for generally the founders of religion speak in the name of the God who is at work in their consciousness of Origin. This kind of speaking may be called "religious" speaking: one could say that God assumes a voice in them. For a Christian all this applies pre-eminently to Christ. Prayer to God and speaking as a

[7] "There are many things which can be conceived only with difficulty, but which are relatively easy to 'live.' In my opinion, prayer continues to be one of them, even though it is true that today more assistance is needed for this purpose than used to be the case in former times." Han M. Fortmann, *Hoogtijd*, Utrecht, 1966, p. 152.

witness for God are two fundamental forms of religious expression that can be found in every type of religion.

4. THE RELATIVITY OF MAN'S IMAGES OF GOD

When speaking to God or in the name of God, man forms an image of God for himself, he has a certain representation of God. Many such representations have succeeded one another in the course of mankind's history. Primitive man had a primitive concept of God, of course, but as man's critical thinking developed, his image of God also became more refined. God was often conceived as a hidden force of nature and even more frequently patterned after man himself. The plurality of man sometimes led to a plural conception of God. Medieval scholastic theodicy, which strongly influenced Descartes, had a much more refined concept of God, but it continued to think of God in terms of a human model: the positive characteristics of man were stripped of their imperfections and then endowed with infinity. If man's field of knowledge was limited by time and space, that of God encompassed everything: God was infinite and limitless consciousness. Undoubtedly, such a concept of God is more refined than others, but it remains a mere image. The more prominent thinkers of the Middle Ages themselves were at least obscurely aware of this fact.[8]

Contemporary religious consciousness is precisely characterized by its profound realization of the fact that we speak in inadequate images about something which cannot be imagined or put into words. Our concept of God may be more refined, but we know that it is a mere image.

[8] Cf. William A. Luijpen, *Phenomenology and Atheism*, Pittsburgh, 1964, p. 336.

And we also know that we will never manage to rise above such a sphere of mere images. For this very reason, however, we are also less afraid to use images. One who imagines that he can transcend the sphere of images and can attain understanding in the strict sense of the term will be inclined to assume an attitude of scorn with respect to inadequate representations. But today we realize that we have nothing but inadequate images;[9] hence we do not feel any intellectual superiority which would make us scorn them. Our religiousness no longer has any objection to a film in which a teacher tells Negro children a story about God and which lets Him appear as a young Negro speaking with Noah. After a period of "'demythologizing," we now again begin to savor "myths." We are no longer afraid of "myths" because we have divested them of the claim that they were supposed to tell us the historical course of affairs in a more or less scientific fashion. We now realize that "myths" present us with a fundamental truth by means of images and that this truth can only be expressed in the form of images. Now that our time has "demythologized" the "myth," we are again able to read the story of creation in the book *Genesis* with reverence and without being embarrassed. We see there man's religious consciousness of Origin presented with beautiful imagery. The "myths" of the New Testament, on the other hand, have not yet been sufficiently "demytholo-

---

[9] "God is a problem. We can no longer imagine God in any other way than as a problem, an empty void caused by the disappearance of the [traditional] image of God. God is no longer anywhere: He is not above us, not outside us, not inside us. Whatever we project or introject is not God. God is a void on the place where an historical idea had located Him. This empty place is a space reserved for Him. God is the void, surrounded by pseudo-gods. Pseudo-gods, broken fragments of our image of God, mark the emptiness aimed at by the question about God." Cornelius Verhoeven, *Rondom de leegte*, Utrecht, 1966, p. 164.

gized" to let everyone read them with the same feeling of reverence and without any embarrassment.

The religious art of our time is certainly not characterized by great freedom in the use of images to express the reality of God. In the past, in the Middle Ages and the Renaissance, there was much more freedom in this matter. The boldness with which the artists then expressed religious reality continues to surprise us. We are thinking here, for example, of the Adoration of the Lamb, the masterpiece of the van Eycks, in the Cathedral of Ghent. Heaven and earth constitute an integral whole dominated by God, in which everything is permeated with His eternal tranquillity. Our entire world—the sky and the soil, flowers, trees and grass, animals and human beings—is there, but everything is deeply marked with the tranquillity of eternity. One would be inclined to speak here of a sublimation of human realities; nevertheless, the religious inspiration of this masterpiece is obvious. An enormous distance separates this kind of religious expression from that of contemporary artists.

What is the reason for this difference? Our artists can no longer visualize the human world in the same way as the van Eycks did. Even the greatest of them do not see the world any longer in that way and, even if they could, they would not be inclined to do it. The reason is not that former ages lived in a time of tranquillity while we are living in a period of crisis. The idea that the Middle Ages were a time of peace is a figment of the imagination: there were no world wars, but local wars, with all the horrors of any war, were very numerous. Must we say perhaps that formerly there existed greater unanimity because so many more things were generally accepted as fixed social achievements and unquestioningly admitted? It is true that today we are much more divided in such matters, but this cannot be the full explanation. In the author's opinion, the explanation should be sought in the above-mentioned fact that modern man is much more conscious of the darkness which permeates all light. Artists especially are very sensitive in this matter and therefore unable to speak in clear and tranquil images about a world which for them is not at all a clear and tranquil world. If this is true, then it follows that they are also unable to express man's religious dimension in a clear and tranquil fashion. In almost every realm the language of art has become hesitant, groping and uncertain of itself. This hesitancy manifests itself not only in the building of churches but also in that of dwellings—at least insofar as the latter are not simply a repetition of old patterns recognized as inadequate. Darkness occurs not only in religious paintings but also in other forms of painting.

In the sphere of theoretical reflection the illusion has sometimes existed that it is possible for man to grasp the religious dimension, not merely in inadequate images but in genuine concepts. It stands to reason that in the sphere of art this illusion could not arise, for the obvious reason that art must always express itself in images. This is why Plato with his love for ideas considered art frivolous. Precisely because art realizes that it must speak in images about the religious dimension, it will embody this dimension in the same general sphere as it uses for other objects. One can make a distinction, of course, between religious and profane art, but there will always be a deep bond between these two because in both the artist expresses himself in images. In his embodiment of the religious dimension, the artist will make use of the same general sphere in which he embodies everything else. Thus it is not surprising that Botticelli's Madonnas and his Birth of Venus show the same style. In a similar way the same darkness can be observed in contemporary expressions of the religious dimension and in those of other dimensions.

The problem of religious expression now returns unsolved. The artist embodies the religious dimension in a way that is connected, identical even, with the way he embodies everything. What, then, makes religious expression different? What makes religious expression religious? Searching for a solution of this problem, one can experience that a path which at first seems to lead to an answer subsequently proves to be a dead end street.

Religion, we saw, is consciousness of Origin. There can be no question of religious expression if this consciousness does not play an essential role in the form or shape used by the artist. But this role can be played in many different ways. The artist can be deeply convinced that the Origin in which he believes is dark, unknown, inaccessible. In this case his religious expression will imply that he shapes things in such a way that their clarity, transparency and obviousness disappears. His expression then becomes religious because the mystery of Origin is reflected by the mysterious character in which he clothes things. The artist will conjure before us an enigmatic world because he expresses the mystery of the Origin in the things themselves. This is what happens especially today.

There exists, however, also a way of expressing religiousness which is almost the exact opposite. It often happens—*happened* would be more correct—that the believer's certainty about the Origin seemed, as it were, to eliminate the ambiguity of our world, that he could place before us a world permeated with the serenity of a superhuman tranquillity. This happens, for example, in the Adoration of the Lamb. The world presented there is not the real medieval world, but a sublimated world in which people appear to us who are raised above the ambiguity of existence. The van Eyck painting presents a world seen, as it were, from the standpoint of the intentions ascribed to it at its origin. It is a world that is more the work of

God than that of men, a world which lies on the other side of human history.

Shortly after its foundation, Christianity began to be a powerful source of inspiration for the artist. Christianity is the doctrine of the Incarnate God: the Origin of everything has appeared among us in a visible form. It is hardly necessary to add that this doctrine does not eliminate the darkness of this Origin. The Bible describes Christ both as the revelation of God's majesty and as a sufferer who obediently empties Himself. In this way Christianity offers inspiration for both of the above-mentioned ways of religious art.

It inspires some artists to sublimation of phenomenal reality. Examples of this trend are found in the old Roman basilicas and the sublime mosaics of Ravenna: the majesty of the Origin inserts itself in history, and man, as conscious of this Origin, is made something sublime. This sublimation affects not only the representation of Christ Himself but also that of the Mother of God and the Saints, in whom Christ's influence is at work. Byzantine and early medieval art give expression to a sublimated humanity. This type of religious expression can perhaps be better understood if we compare it with so-called socialistic art. The latter is usually said to be realistic; nevertheless, it also implies a sublimation or idealization. Socialism transcends the man who *is* in terms of the ideal of the man who ought to be. Socialistic art, therefore, presents us with the man who ought to be and who is predelineated in the present. It claims that the man who ought to be is the social man, the "hero" of work. In medieval themes of artistic expression there exists certainly as much regularity as in the socialistic schema. In both, certain topics are unendingly repeated. As compared to medieval art, however, the socialistic sublimation is poor and boring. Socialism has not succeeded in inspiring its artists to the grandeur of forms which we find in the early Middle Ages.

The figure of the suffering Christ inspired a form of art expressing the *kenosis*.[10] This art is centered on the Cross. We encounter here the darkness of destruction and death, but it is not a death without hope. The annihilation is accepted in trust, though the suffering and pain do not thereby become less. This motif reveals itself not only in the representation of Christ but also in that of His Mother and His followers. Here also the consciousness of Origin is at work: destruction, suffering and death are seen, as was their sublimation, as a continuation of the Origin in human history.

5. THE QUESTION OF AUTHENTICITY

The creator of religious art embodies man's consciousness of Origin in his work. This consciousness influences everything he produces without ever itself becoming apparent. It makes things appear without appearing itself. Religious art gives form and shape to something which itself cannot appear as a form. That in the perspective of which everything is expressed is not itself expressed. Without the consciousness of Origin that existed in Antiquity and the Middle Ages in the Church, the artistic forms embodying this consciousness would never have been created. Yet, it is true that the ground from which all these visible forms arose remains itself invisible. No expert will deny that in this matter a distinction must be made between the authentic and the inauthentic. Just as not every

---

[10] In his book, *The Church is Different*, New York, 1967, Robert Adolfs argues that the Church of the future must place itself in the perspective of the *kenosis*. He refers to this Church as the kenotic Church.

book containing philosophical topics is authentic philosophy, so also we must say that not every work of art which represents a religious topic is religious art. In practice, however, it is extremely difficult to maintain this distinction. Is, for example, the St. Peter's Church of Rome an authentically religious work of art? Should Botticelli's Madonnas be called authentically religious paintings? Discussions about such questions are likely to last forever.

This phenomenon, however, occurs in all realms. There exists, for instance, a dispute about what "authentic" philosophy is. Adherents of linguistic analysis think that many continental European publications in philosophy are not authentically philosophical because their use of language is not sufficiently critical. In the eyes of analytic philosophers those works are mere "literature." The continental philosophers, on the other hand, argue that the English thinkers with their detailed analyses do not really reach the fundamental philosophical questions. What is authentic philosophy? what is authentic art? what is authentic morality? what is authentic humanity? According to Marxists, there can be no question of authentic humanity as long as one does not decisively go against man's so-called self-alienations. But Western man argues that in Marxist countries humanity is sacrificed on the altar of a system. All this shows that it is not only in religious art that the question is asked as to what is authentic and what inauthentic. Obviously, the question will always remain difficult to answer. But this does not allow us to conclude that "therefore" religious art does not exist—no more than we are permitted to argue from the other disputes that authentic philosophy, authentic art, humanity and morality do not exist. In our opinion, there is religious expression, religious art when the religious consciousness of Origin is at work in the forms of expression or of art. And, as we saw, the influence of this consciousness can manifest itself either by eliminating clarity because of the darkness of the Origin or by sublimating the forms because of the grandeur of this Origin.

The accelerated movement of history causes difficulties in man's expressive life. Formerly artists had the time to seek new forms. It took centuries, for example, to find the gothic style of cathedrals, but the necessary time was available because generations came and went without the discovery of new materials or new tools for building churches. In former ages the climax generally came after a long period of common preparation: those who produced the supreme achievements could base themselves on a long tradition which had not yet become antiquated. Today, however, changes occur at a very fast rate so that there is hardly time to develop a tradition which can culminate in superior achievements. In many respects modern man is not yet used to the accelerated tempo of life, but at the same time, he is neither able nor willing to return to the old, more leisurely tempo.

When modern man constructs a building, he plans a more or less accurate "life expectancy" for his construction. A skyscraper is planned to be useful for forty years: after that, new inventions will make the building obsolete. Medieval man, on the other hand, built in a timeless perspective: his palaces and cathedrals did not take obsolescence into account. This difference in perspective obviously has consequences for the form assumed by man's endeavors. The way contemporary man builds is much more functional and utilitarian, and much less concerned with other aspects of form. Modern man refuses to fix his form: he wishes to remain uncommitted with respect to the future because he knows that the future will be different from the present.

All this means that religious expression finds itself in a different atmosphere. In the past it was permeated with the eternal, the everlasting aspect of the Origin. This everlastingness, however, was not diametrically opposed to the atmosphere of daily life, for the later developed only very slowly and thus also seemed to be forever the same. "Actualism" played no role in religious expression: an established form could remain meaningful and acceptable for centuries. The situation is no longer the same today, although some people find it difficult to resign themselves to this fact. But their refusal to recognize this fact and to draw the consequences from it can only make religious expression an anachronism. When human life is subject to fast changes in many realms, religious expression cannot remain aloof from this accelerated tempo of development and stick to the ancient forms. We must find today new forms for expressing our consciousness of Origin, forms that are suitable for the man of today, and we must realize that the forms we find will not be destined to have a long life.

While religious man regards the Origin as eternal, his consciousness of Origin is temporal, and it is this temporal consciousness which gives rise to the forms of his religious expression. The forms do not arise in the eternal God but in temporal man, and this man in our time has become temporal in a new way. This new temporal consciousness must reveal itself in the forms of his expression. Some people experience a nostalgia for the tranquillity of former ages: they would like to preserve this tranquillity, which is already "lost" in many realms, in the realm of religious expression. But it is wrong to think and plan nostalgically in terms of a past that has been overtaken by history. When secular buildings are constructed to last forty years, one should not continue to plan churches to last forever. The man of the future will differ from the man of today, and we have no right to bind him to our ways. Churches must no longer be built with a medieval mentality, i.e., a state of mind which is not in keeping with the accelerated tempo of modern life. Obviously we do not mean that today we may build no monument to last for an indefinite future, but our functional buildings for religious worship should not, as a matter of principle, be constructed as such enduring monuments.

The Roman liturgy in use in the Catholic Church originated in the very distant past and has functioned for many centuries. Today we speak of a "new liturgy," but this new liturgy is not likely to last very long. Less than a decade ago we still used a liturgy more than a thousand years old, but the liturgy we are making now is not destined to endure for centuries. The accelerated rate of obsolescence common to almost every realm of life obviously must be taken into account in our planning of a new liturgy.

Religious expression is not at all dead. Some religious books become bestsellers, and religious events constitute part of news which makes headlines throughout the world. It remains true, nevertheless, that religion is no longer the center of life in the same way as it used to be in the past. For man has made a discovery which seems to be of a definitive nature, viz., the fact that religion cannot supply him with the norms he needs for building his world. This statement needs to be rendered more precise. It refers to the inner organization of the various realms of human endeavor and to the interconnection between these realms. We cannot deduce from man's religious dimension how we must pursue science, how the technical world of labor must be developed, how the economy must be organized, or what connection there is between science and technology, agriculture and industry. Man has discovered himself as a self-project: he himself is the builder and organizer of his world. He himself must seek his ways: they are not given to him by God's revelation.

Nature is not so much a fixed order as a manipulable datum. In former times man saw nature as a firmly established order which had its origin in God and in which man had to insert himself. Thus it was possible then to think that the religious dimension could supply norms for all kinds of human endeavors. Man had not yet been discovered as a self-project. But according as man made progress in this discovery, he gradually also escaped from the supposed control of religious norms. The term "secularization" is often used to indicate this discovery of man as self-project.[11]

In another respect, however, religion continues to hold its ground. Man makes a self-project of himself, but he *finds* this fundamental possibility, it is something *given* to him. Man may be original in his self-project, but his originality is a dependent way of being-original. One could say that man is called to be origin—it does not matter whether one thinks here of a call coming from God or of a destiny implied in his own nature. In either case man looks upon himself as the executor of a call. Consciousness of being called to accomplish such a vocation is just as strong among Marxists as it is among Christians. All this implies that man is confronted with the meaning of being-origin, the meaning of his self-project. Each one has to ask himself how he must situate himself with respect to the world and his fellowmen. This *how* does not refer to a technical question but to the way of looking at life in terms of meaning. Religion cannot supply a meaningful answer to the question how science or technology must be pursued, but religion can speak meaningfully with respect to the way one situates himself in regard to the pursuit of science and technology: religion does not

[11] The consequences of this discovery are developed by Paul van Buren in his well-known work, *The Secular Meaning of the Gospel*, London, 1963.

tell us how we should work, but how we can integrate our work with life.

Secularization is not a threat to religion: it merely eliminates religious interference in matters where religion has no business. Today we are able to make many distinctions in this matter which were beyond the reach of former ages. All this is a gain, not a loss. Religion cannot tell man how he must technically develop his world, but it can busy itself with the question of the meaning this development has for man and how man should situate himself in this technical world.

A consequence of all this is that religion has disappeared from the institutes of research, factories and offices, business districts and recreational areas. Religious forms of expression do not belong there. But religion continues to exist in the human being who situates himself in all this. We continue to provide buildings where people can gather to nourish their religious inspiration, but these buildings need no longer dominate the town or city. Life no longer runs its course in the shadow of the cathedral or local church. These edifices still serve as gathering places where people meet to reflect together on life, which in its inner structures is religionless. Thus it stands to reason that these centers of reflection now occupy a less central and more marginal location.

One could say that religion remains the heart of life, without being its clearly perceptible outer center. During the religious gathering people reflect upon the ultimate meaning of everything, but not in order to regulate everything in terms of religion. How things are to be regulated is something that man must learn elsewhere than in religion. Thus religious expression continues to retain a place, even though it no longer occupies the visible center of expressive life as it used to do in the past.

Religious expression also is a "creation which is at the

same time an adequation." Man acts creatively in it, but in this creation he attempts to give form to the hidden Origin of everything and to his dependence on this Origin. Nowhere, however, are Merleau-Ponty's above-quoted words as ambiguous as here.[12] Religious expression is highly inadequate. It is a privilege of our time that we are conscious of this inadequacy without, however—let us hope—losing sight of the value of religious expression.

[12] Merleau-Ponty does not write about religious expression either in his earlier period when he was estranged from religion or in his last years when he came again closer to religion.

Conclusion

The preceding study of expression remains incomplete. It could hardly be otherwise, for expression is one of the most fundamental phenomena of human life. There exists no genuinely human activity which is not in one way or another a form of expression.

Incomplete as it is, our study possesses unity because it is permeated with one and the same fundamental thought, viz., Merleau-Ponty's idea that man makes reality be for himself through his creative act of expression. Generally speaking, we do not primarily express ourselves but, as intentional beings, we are in the world even in our expressive life. When man himself is the object of his expression, he tries to objectify himself, his attention is centered then on the object-ego and not on the subject-ego who is expressing himself. This idea harmonizes with Merleau-Ponty's view of man, for he refers to man as that part of reality in which and through which reality brings itself to light and which, thus, sets itself apart from reality as a subject.

For this reason we had to object to a view which conceives expression too narrowly by, e.g., excluding science from it. Such a view is wrong because scientific expression occupies a place of the greatest importance in modern life.

Many chapters could have been added to this book, but we paid attention only to a few fundamental truths about expression and analyzed only in a partial way one or two forms of expressive life. Our sole purpose was to offer a philosophical introduction to a topic which needs to be developed more fully by specialists in the various forms of expression. There is need for such a philosophical introduction because the phenomenon of expression must be seen within the context of man's whole existence.

Index of Names and Subject Matter